PATENT LAW

PATENT LAW
for Scientists, Inventors & Business Management

by
Bruce Stein, R.Ph., Ph.D., J.D.
Patent Attorney

Kp

Kalamazoo Publishing
2013

Kalamazoo Publishing
Kalamazoo, Michigan, USA, 49009
www.kazoopub.com

ISBN 978-0-9831991-4-4

Stein, Bruce
    Patent law for scientists, inventors & business management. Kalamazoo, Mich.: Kalamazoo Publishing, 2013.
    xx, 156 pp.   Includes index
    1. Patent law and legislation—United States
2. U.S. Patent and Trademark Office I. Title

348.732 S8191   KF2974.6 S9191

Prepublication services: Words by Design

DEDICATION

This book is dedicated to all those individuals and businesses that worked so hard, spent so much time and effort, invested so much capital doing research and development only to find that the patent that they thought would give them exclusivity is either easy for competitors to work around or is invalid, rendering their efforts of little or no value.

Hopefully, this book will help prevent such unfortunate tragic errors.

CONTENTS

FIGURES

TABLES

PREFACE

It is truly tragic to see inventors, scientists and businesses invest thousands of hours of time and large amounts of financial resources in research to develop a commercially viable product, composition or process, only to see the inventor/assignee unable to exclude others from the invention. This occurs when third parties legally use the inventive concept by working around the claims or invalidating the patent.

We are all aware of how complex the tax code is and the necessary assistance of knowledgeable individuals in preparing income tax forms. With personal income taxes if one can not file on time, you just apply for an automatically granted extension. If an individual or corporation makes an error, you can file an amended return. However, procedurally patent law is not so forgiving and substantively it is equally or more complex.

Procedurally, in most cases if you miss a filing date or due date by just one day, you can lose all patent rights. Substantively, one of the more fundamentally basic concepts of patent law—that a patent does not give the owner the right to use the claimed invention, but only the right to exclude others—is not generally understood. Both corporate executives and patent administrators who are responsible for and make critical decisions about patents and investing often do not have sufficient knowledge of substantive patent law to make well informed business decisions.

This book is a compilation of my "Patent Law for Scientists and Management" short course which I have presented for about 30 years, coast to coast. The short course was started because The Upjohn Company many years ago lost a patent opportunity on a very important commercial process. If a division of a major pharmaceutical company which was extensively involved in research and patenting for over 90 years and whose VP had many patents in his own name could lose a patent opportunity, then it could and does happen all the time to those less experienced.

About 1980 I received a phone call from Dr. A.W. Schneider a VP at The Upjohn Company.[1] Dr. Schneider had a number of patents as an inventor and was VP of Research & Development of the Fine Chemical Division of Upjohn. This division was responsible for doing research to improve the process chemistry in making active ingredients for pharmaceutical products and intermediates for sale. Dr. Schneider relayed that there was an excellent process that they had been using for about two or three years, and he wanted it patented. The Upjohn Company had been receiving tons of soy sterols as a by-product of the soy industry and wanted to use the sterols as a very cheap starting material in the production of pharmaceutically useful corticoids and progesterones. To accomplish that, the chemists had to find a way to cleave the exocyclic Δ^{22}-double bond without cleaving the endocyclic Δ^5-double bond of the steroid B-ring. Dr. Schneider related

[1] The Upjohn Company (Upjohn) merged with Pharmacia to become Pharmacia and Upjohn, then Pharmacia. It was later acquired by Pfizer.

that the Upjohn chemists working on the project were unable to do the selective cleavage.

Fortunately, one day a professor from a major university chemistry department was at Upjohn for a seminar and when asked by the chemist working on the project for a suggestion on how to selectively cleave the desired double bond, the professor suggested a particular catalyst. It worked quantitatively. Upjohn was so pleased that they sent the professor a $5,000 check, quickly scaled up the process and put it in commercial production. Now Dr. Schneider wanted the process patented.

I responded that there were three major problems with patenting the process. First, since Upjohn had used the process commercially for more than one year, under 35 U.S.C.[2] §102, it was no longer patentable by Upjohn. Second, from the little information that I was given, it appeared that professor was the inventor (or certainly a co-inventor) of the process and third, why did Upjohn send the professor $5,000 gratuitously without asking the professor to assign his rights in the invention to Upjohn?

Dr. Schneider quickly acknowledged that Fine Chemicals had made three very costly errors. To prevent future occurrences of costly errors like this, Dr. Schneider asked me to prepare an educational patent law program for scientists and management, and to present it regularly to the Fine Chemical division. So began "Patent Law for Scientists and Management." As I learned of other errors Upjohn scientists and/or management were making, or were likely to make, I added that material to my course. The course expanded over the years to a half-day program which I

---

[2] U.S.C. refers to United States Code (federal statutory law). Title 35 is patent law.

have presented coast to coast. It is the material from that program that I have presented here as *Patent Law for Scientists, Investors & Business Management* so you are less likely to make mistakes in obtaining patents.

Having read and studied the material in this book will not make you an expert or competent to draft, file or prosecute a patent application. This book is not intended as a comprehensive teaching of all patent law. Rather it is intended to educate the reader on issues which I have found (1) to be critical to good patent protection and (2) which the scientist and/or management person involved can have some influence over. The book will give you sufficient information to understand the important issues in the patent process and to communicate intelligently with your patent attorney. You are the client and should make some of the decisions often made by the patent attorney by default because the inventor/scientist or management person involved has no knowledge of the issue. Make sure you understand the issues and alternatives available to you before starting to apply for a patent.

Do not hesitate to ask questions if you do not understand. If you have any questions, contact your patent attorney.

Let's begin our journey into the complex territory where technology, law and business not only meet but overlap. Each area has its own language and critically important issues. You know the technology of your invention. This book aims to educate you about legal and business issues that cause scientists, inventors and business management to make costly errors in trying to obtain patents for their technology so you can be successful in developing and commercializing your invention.

Unique Organization of This Book

In a book about patents, the subject matter in the first chapter following the book's introductory chapter is almost always related to how the reader should proceed to obtain a patent. That is why all of you are reading this book; to answer the question, "How do I obtain a patent on my invention?" However, I respectfully dissent and have made the first chapter after the introduction, a chapter on freedom to operate.

My reason is simple. You do not need a patent to market a product or practice a process. However, you do need freedom to operate. When clients come to me wanting me to patent their invention, I first ask them, "Do you have freedom to operate?" They usually respond, "What?"

Before you can think of patenting your invention, you need to make sure you are not infringing the patent of another. Even if your invention is patentable, if you are infringing the patent of a third party you will not be able to market your (patentable) invention without a license from the third-party patentee. If they will not grant you the license, you will not be able to commercialize your invention regardless if you obtain a patent on it.

If your invention is a motor which makes a lawnmower run more efficiently, let's assume you will obtain a patent on (1) the more efficient motor and (2) on a lawnmower containing that motor. Assuming you want to use the state-of-the-art parts in your lawnmower, they must be patent free. If the state of the art brake system is patented by a third party, you will not be able to make, use or sell the lawnmower using the patented clutch because you would be infringing the patent of the assignee of the clutch (absent a license to do so). You would not have "freedom to operate."

From a legal perspective, you can make, use and sell a lawnmower with your more efficient motor using an older patent-free clutch. However, from a business perspective, that is not desirable. In the real world what usually occurs is cross licensing where you agree to license the assignee of the clutch patent rights to use the more efficient motor and the assignee of the clutch patent licenses you the right to use the patented clutch during the life of the patent. The licenses are not co-extensive because the patent on the clutch will expire before the patent on your improved motor. After the clutch patent expires and you are free to use it without royalty payment, you will still receive a royalty payment until your patent expires.

In some cases, rather than both of you competing on the market, you would just license the competitor in exchange for a royalty payment. In Chapter II, "Freedom to Operate," actual examples describe parties who obtained patents but did not have freedom to operate. That will help you understand this issue better.

Once you have determined whether or not you have freedom to operate, then you can move on to the issue of patentability of your invention. All the searching you have done to determine whether or not you have freedom to operate is very useful in helping determine whether your invention is likely to be patentable.

Not infrequently in doing a search to determine freedom to operate, inventors find that they do not have freedom to operate because a patent exists claiming their exact invention. Hence, the invention is not novel and therefore not patentable. Further, they cannot make, use[3] or sell it because

---

[3] Under the America Invents Act of 2011, you have "prior user rights" and can make and use the invention for *personal use* if you had been using the invention before the patentee filed. You can not transfer that right.

they would be infringing the existing patent. Making sure one has freedom to operate before taking up patentability of one's invention is putting the horse before the cart.

Acknowledgements

The author would very much like to thank those who read and provided helpful comments and suggestions regarding the draft of this book, in particular Paul Collins, Ph.D. (former Senior Research Fellow at G.D. Searle & Co), Paul Aristoff, Ph.D. (former Director of Medicinal Chemistry at Pharmacia, David Hackstadt, M.D. (staff physician at Tampa General Hospital emergency room) and Elbert Roberts (former patent examiner at the USPTO).

In addition, the author would like to thank Ellen Nelson for her front cover concept.

Since this book is based heavily on my short course, "Patent Law for Scientists and Management," the author would also like to thank all those who took the short course and further took the time to offer comments and suggestions for improving it.

I.
INTRODUCTION

Patents as Intellectual Property

Intellectual property (IP) includes patents, trademarks, copyrights and trade secrets. Patents which contain intellectual property are documents issued by governments of virtually all industrialized nations following an application and examination process.

Patents include utility patents, design and plant patents. Design patents are used to protect decorative designs. Design patents are granted to an inventor who invents a new, original and ornamental design for an article of manufacture. They are of limited value because of they are limited to just one claim. I have never drafted or prosecuted one.

A trademark is a brand name. It includes any word, name, symbol, device, or any combination, used or intended to be used to identify and distinguish the goods/services of one seller or provider from those of others and to indicate the source of the goods/services. It does not preclude selling the same or similar product under a different name by a different vendor.

Copyrights are for books, music, movies, etc., and are limited to copying.

Trade secrets can be valuable for processes and novel microorganisms, but offer little or no protection for products which can be reverse engineered. The advantage of trade secrets is that they do not expire after twenty years as do patents. The Coca-Cola trade secret is still a trade secret after half a century.

Plant patents are granted to anyone who invents or discovers and asexually reproduces any distinct and new variety of plant. Plant patents are distinct from Plant Variety Protection Certificates.[4]

Utility Patent Subjects

The term "utility patent" refers to what non-patent attorneys call "patents." The term "provisional" refers to patent applications and not issued patents. Provisional patent applications are patent applications that are filed with the Untied States Patent and Trademark Office (USPTO) to establish an early filing date. The applicant(s) must file a regular utility patent application within one year to be able to claim the date of the provisional application and obtain a U.S. patent. The United States is the only country to use provisional patent applications.

While the Federal Patent Statute (35 U.S.C.) and the Code of Federal Regulations for patents (37 C.F.R.) treat all utility patents the same, their technical subject matter can be subdivided into three categories. Types of subject matter that can be claimed in each catagory:

---
[4] 7 U.S.C. §2321–2582

CHEMICAL[5]
    Compounds (antibiotics, anti-AIDS drugs,
        cholesterol-lowering, or erectile
        dysfunction (ED) pharmaceuticals)
    Crystal forms (new forms of known
        compounds)
    Processes
        chemical transformations
        physical processes (producing
          microcrystals of known compound)
        biological processes (fermentations,
          cell-free enzymatic reactions,
          medical screens, e.g., breast cancer
            gene tests,
          treatment methods in humans
            and animals)
    Compositions
        ointments, tablets, creams
        IV bags
        car polishes
        weed killers and fertilizers

MECHANICAL
    Equipment
    Carburetors
    Modified endotracheal tubes
    Pumps
    Tools
    New processes with old equipment or
        tools

ELECTRICAL
    New items
    Group of items (different arrangement of
        same items)
    Processes

---

[5] Because I am a pharmacist, my Ph.D. is in fermentation chemistry and I spent more than 25 years as a patent attorney with a pharmaceutical company, most of my examples and illustrations will be chemical.

This list is far from complete, but gives a good idea of what is possible to be claimed in a patent. The claims of the patent give the owner of the patent the rights the owner acquires.

What Are Claims and Why Are They Important?

Claims are the part of a patent application which gives the owner property rights. Claims are to patents, what meets and bounds are to real property or a title is to a car. Since it is the claims which give the owner specific property rights, the claims are of crucial importance to the value of a patent. An introduction to claims will be discussed here so the reader fully understands issues that follow.

Once a patent application and/or PCT[6] application has been filed the claims cannot be broadened. They can be cancelled or narrowed by amendment, but not broadened, so it is extremely important that the claims be filed in as broad a scope as the applicant needs to cover these aspects:

1. What the applicant desires to do,

2. Ways in which third-party competitors would like to use the invention without infringing to compete with the applicant (*see* Chapter IV),

3. Subject matter the applicant may not want to use, but which can be licensed for royalty income.

The following will demonstrate the importance of correctly worded claims. A more thorough discussion of the claims and not losing patent

[6] PCT refers to the Patent Cooperation Treaty, an international treaty regarding the filing and prosecution of patent applications in countries around the world.

rights by having third parties use the invention (by working around the wording of the claims) is set forth in Chapter IV, "How Not to Lose Your Patent Rights."

Frank Farmer majored in agronomic farming and minored in chemistry when in college. Frank now farms soybeans and troublesome weeds are substantially reducing his yields. When he used known herbicides, they injured his crop and reduced his yield. To solve this problem Frank modified the herbicide and developed "X" that does not injure his soybean crop, the vegetables in his garden or his lawn. Realizing the value of what he had, Frank rushed to a patent attorney and informed the patent attorney he wanted a provisional patent application filed immediately. The patent attorney promptly filed a provisional, in due course a PCT application and then U.S. national phase application. Finally a patent issued; the broadest claim in Frank's patent was what he desired to do, "A herbicide of formula X for use with soybeans."

As a good business man Frank licensed Agricultural Chemicals to produce and sell the new herbicide with directions that it can be used with soybeans without injuring the plants nor reducing the yield. In addition to income from farming his soybean crop which now has better yields, Frank now also receives royalties from the licensee. In due course Frank realized that Agricultural Chemicals was selling a lot more product than they were paying him royalties for. As a good business man he went to discuss the matter with the Director of Licensing for Agricultural Chemicals.

Frank asked, "Was not Agricultural Chemicals now selling a lot more product?" and "Why were they not paying him a coextensive increased amount of royalties?" The Director readily admitted that they were selling more and, that under the license agreement, Agricultural Chemicals was only obligated to pay Frank a royalty for sales which would infringe his patent. Further, the Director explained, most of the sales were for other agronomic crops, such as cotton, corn, tobacco and peanuts, and these items were not within the scope of the claim to Frank's patent. Therefore, they did not owe him any royalty.

Frank pointed out to the Director that in the specification[7] of his patent, it is stated that the novel herbicide X can be used with other crops, flowers and on lawns. The Director acknowledged this but stated that the specification does not provide any property rights—only the claims do—and the claim in the patent is limited to soybeans. Use of X with commercial plants other than soybeans does not infringe the patent and Agricultural Chemicals does not owe Frank a royalty for these sales. Unhappy with this explanation, Frank went to see his patent attorney who verified that the Director was correct. Frank asked what he could now do to add other agronomic crops to his patent. The patent attorney said there was nothing he could do now. The claim had to be worded correctly as filed in the original patent application and once filed cannot be broadened.

Frank then inquired of the patent attorney as to why he did not include other agronomic crops, vegetable or flowers or grass (lawns) in the claims. The attorney responded that Frank had never informed him that those items were important. Further, when he asked Frank to proofread the entire patent application, both specification and claims, prior to filing, Frank had indicated that

---

[7] The specification is the non-claim portion of the patent.

everything was fine.[8] He reminded Frank that Frank never indicated that he wanted to include other items in the claims for purposes of licensing. Many options on how to word the claim were originally possible:

> "A herbicide of formula X for use with agronomic crops." If this choice had been used, Frank would have received royalties on sales of "X" for use on all agronomic crops, but not for vegetable crops.

> "A herbicide of formula X for use with agronomic and vegetable crops." With this wording, Frank would have received royalties on sales of "X" for use on all agronomic and vegetable crops, but not for use around fruits, such as strawberries, blueberries, cherries, etc.

> "A herbicide of formula X for use with all edible crops." Had the claim been worded this way, Frank would have received royalties on sales of "X" for use on all agronomic, vegetable and fruit crops, but not for use around flowering plants.

> "A herbicide of formula X for use with commercially important plants selected from the group consisting of agronomic crops, vegetables, fruits and flowering plants." This way Frank would have received royalties on sales of "X" for use on all of the above, but not for use on lawns.

> "A herbicide of formula X." Frank would have received royalties on all sales of "X" regardless of the use with this option.

---

[8] This is an extremely common error. It occurs because patentees do not understand that patents do not give the assignee the right to use the claimed invention, but only the right to exclude others. The purpose of a claim is to encompass conduct of others that you want to prohibit.

The simplest claim on what Frank desired to do, "1. A herbicide of formula X," is the broadest since it does not have any use limitation. Any sale or use of it infringes Frank's patent and he would receive a royalty on *all* sales.

From the above you can see how critical it is for a claim to be worded properly. While the applicant wants the broadest claim that can be obtained, it can not be so broad as to include inoperable subject matter.

Why Obtain Patents?

Reasons for obtaining patents depends on who you are. Large corporations and some smaller businesses usually obtain patents to have true market exclusivity. They want to be the only ones in the market being able to sell their product or composition or use a specific process because if they are the only ones, there is much less (price) competition. Many large corporations obtain patents and never work them, they use them solely in a defensive manner to keep their competition from being able to use the patented subject matter. It is very much like certain businesses, like gas stations or fast food places, purchasing desirable corner lots or places near interstate highways to prevent competition from moving in by purchasing them and becoming a direct competitor.

Universities, sole inventors and most small businesses usually obtain patents with no intention of ever making or selling the product or composition or using the process. Rather they develop something that others want and are willing to pay for. These entities then try to license the patent application before the big expense in patent prosecution (all the steps following the filing of a provisional application up until the patent issues) occurs at just before the 30-month mark.

Some small businesses and sole inventors use patents to try and obtain venture capital, the patent application being their asset. The problem is that a patent application is just that, an application, it may never develop into a patent or even if it does, the scope of the claims may be substantially reduced.

Lastly there are some who want to obtain patents to add to their CV, just as they add publications. They believe because it is different from a publication and more related to the real commercial world, it is equal or better than a publication.

The inability of sole inventors and very small businesses to develop and market products successfully is well known. At meetings of inventors, small businesses and investors where the inventors and small businesses are seeking funding, when investors ask the question, "What is your exit strategy?" they are looking for the answer, "Out license." They do not want to hear, "We will produce and sell."

What Rights Do Patents Give the Owner?

Patents give the owner (assignee) or licensee the right to exclude others from making, using, selling, importing or offering for sale the claimed invention. The patent owner has the right to exclude others from the above activities for a period of 20 years from the date of filing of the patent application (approximately 21 years from the filing date of the provisional patent application) for subject matter in the scope of the allowed claims.

The thing to note, that most miss and do not understand about patent law, is that the patent owner does *not* have the right to use the claimed invention by virtue of having a patent; only *the right to exclude others* from using the claimed invention. While this may not make sense, below are some examples that will help you understand this crucially important concept. First one important comment, the allowed claims can never be broader than the claims as filed and often are narrower because of either amendments to the claims or canceling claims.

Real World Examples

To help you better understand the important concept that *a patent does NOT give the owner (assignee) or licensee the right to use the claimed invention but rather only the right to exclude others,* I will provide a number of examples which illustrate this.

With FREEDOX, Pharmacia patented the compound, a commercial process and three formulations (see Table 1). The utility was for CNS trauma, such as stroke, head injury, subarachnoid hemorrhage, spinal cord injury, etc. InSite Vision's patent claimed a method of using FREEDOX for ophthalmic use. Even though InSite has a patent for the use of FREEDOX for ophthalmic use, it could not make, use or sell FREEDOX for ophthalmic use because it would infringe Pharmacia's 281 patent. Likewise, Pharmacia could not offer for sale or sell FREEDOX for ophthalmic use because it would infringe InSite's patent. So neither Pharmacia nor InSite could sell FREEDOX for ophthalmic use without a license from the other.

Similarly, with regard to the subject matter of International Publication WO96/15795. Pharmacia could not offer for sale or sell FREEDOX for preventing surgical adhesions because it would infringe on the patent resulting from International Publication WO96/15795, and the University of California, or their licensee, could not sell FREEDOX for surgical adhesions because it would infringe Pharmacia's 281 patent.

Table 1. FREEDOX **(tirilazad mesylate) Patents Granted.**

Patent No.	Claimed Subject Matter	Assignee
5,175,281	Compound – tirilazad	Pharmacia
5,225,555	Commercial Process →tirilazad	Pharmacia
4,968,675	Rx[9] composition – citrate	Pharmacia
5,858,999	Rx composition – co-solvent	Pharmacia
6,531,139	Rx composition – emulsion	Pharmacia
5,124,154	Method of Use[10] – ophthalmic	InSite Vision
WO96/15795	Method of Use – surgical adhesion	U of Calif.

In both situations any third party interested in marketing FREEDOX for ophthalmic use or in preventing surgical adhesions would need a license from both parties.

Other examples on rights obtained by patents are illustrated with tipranavir and minoxidil (see Tables 2 and 3):

---

[9] Rx is an abbreviation for pharmacy, pharmaceutical, etc.
[10] A method of use (MOT) patent is a process patent. It involves steps just as a chemical, mechanical or electrical process, but only when in humans or useful warm-blooded mammals.

Table 2. Tipranavir Patents Granted.

Patent No.	Claimed Subject Matter	Assignee
5,852,195	Compound – Tipranavir genus	Pharmacia
6,169,181	Compound – tipranavir species	Pharmacia
5,840,751	Compound –	Warner Lambert

Pharmacia's patents claim both a genus and the species, tipranavir, an anti-AIDS pharmaceutical. Warner Lambert's 751 patent claimed similar compounds.

Tipranavir has the chemical structural formula which has two asymmetric centers as shown in Figure 1:

Figure 1. Tipranavir Structural Formula.

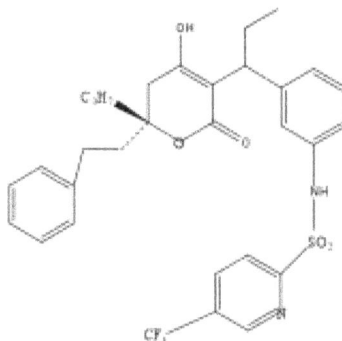

An asymmetric center is a carbon atom with four different groups attached producing two enantiomers (isomers), one "left handed" and one "right handed" which are mirror images of each other (see Appendix A for a graphic demonstration). With two asymmetric centers there are four isomers. At the bench level, cost of synthesis is not a concern. However, once tipranavir became a commercial AIDS drug, it was much tooooooooo expensive to produce by the bench process. A new process was invented to produce tipranavir in commercial quantities at a reasonable cost.

Figure 2. Substituent Compounds Claimed by Warner Lambert's Patent.

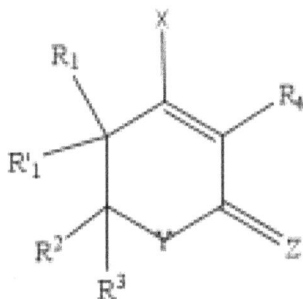

The variable substituents on tipranavir, X, R_1, R_2, ..., Z, were defined by the patentee to produce tipranavir commercially. They included a compound within the scope of a claim in the Warner Lambert patent when the variable substituents are these chemical groups:

> where X is –OH;
> where Z is =O;
> where R_1 and R'_1 are each independently $[CH_2]n_1$-$[W_1]n_2$-$[Ar]n_2$-$[CH_2]n_3$-$[W_2]n_4$-R_7
> where R_4 is $[CH_2]n_1$-$[W_3]n_2$-$[W_4]n_4$-$[Ar]n_2$-$[CH_2]n_3$-$[W_2]n_4$-R_7

All of these substituents are within the scope of one or more of the claims of the Warner Lambert patent. This meant when Pharmacia produced tipranavir by their commercial process, Pharmacia would be infringing the Warner Lambert patent. Hence, even though Pharmacia had not one, but two patents claiming tipranavir, they could not sell it because they could not make it without infringing the patent of a third party. I solved this problem by obtaining a license from Warmer Lambert to "use" their compound as an intermediate.

Table 3. ROGAINE (minoxidil) Patents Granted.

Patent No.	Claimed Subject Matter	Assignee
3,461,461	Compound – Minoxidil	Upjohn
4,139,619	MOT – minoxidil to grow hair	C & K[11]
4,596,812	MOT – minoxidil to grow hair	C & K

The Upjohn Company patented minoxidil and marketed it in tablet form to treat hypertension. Two physicians—Chidsey and Kahn—observed that some of their patients who were taking minoxidil were growing hair. Realizing they had found a pharmaceutical that will grow hair, they patented the use of minoxidil to grow hair.

Even though Upjohn had a patent on minoxidil, they could not sell it to grow hair because they would infringe the C & K patents. Chidsey and Kahn could not sell minoxidil in topical form to grow hair because they would infringe the Upjohn patent. This situation was resolved with Upjohn selling ROGAINE and paying the two doctors a royalty.

A final example involves gene transfer:

Table 4. Cohen Boyer Patent.

Patent No.	Claimed Subject Matter	Assignee
4,237,224	Process – gene transfer	Stanford U

The Cohen Boyer patent is a biological process for which claim 1 reads:

A method for replicating a biologically functional DNA, which comprises:

---

[11] The facts are not exactly as set forth here because of various legal procedures not relevant to this discussion. However, it is an excellent teaching example using a well-known product.

(a) transforming compatible unicellular organisms with biologically functional DNA to form transformants;

(b) cleaving a viral or circular plasmid DNA to provide a first linear segment having an intact replicon and termini of a predetermined character;

(c) combining said first linear segment with a second linear DNA segment;

(d) growing said unicellular organisms under appropriate nutrient conditions; and

(e) isolating transformants by means of phenotypical trait imparted by biologically functional DNA.

This is an extremely broad claim which is permitted in a virgin area of science. An agricultural scientist who invented and patented a way to transfer a drought-resistant gene from cactus to a crop like corn would infringe this patent. Similarly, an environmental scientist who invented and patented a way to transfer an oil-metabolizing gene to bacterial colonies to eat oil slicks would also infringe this patent. Almost any invention involving gene transfer would likely infringe the Cohen Boyer patent.

So, all these scientists with their own patents would not be able to use their inventions without a license from Stanford. It is my understanding that licenses were granted to all small businesses who wanted one for the nominal amount of $10,000.

Property Rights Compared

For the most part, patent rights are similar to real property (RP) and personal property (PP) rights (*see* Table 5), but there are three big differences:

1. Patents expire 20 years from the date of the PCT application (about 21 years after the filing of the provisional patent application).

Your RP (house), car and other PP can be retained as long as you desire.

2. Only one party can own your house or car, whereas more than one party can claim patentable subject matter. This leads to the situation where each can prevent the other from using it. If you own your house or car, a third party can not prevent you from using or selling it.

3. Once you own your house/lot and car it is yours. During a patent trial on the issue of validity a court can declare one or all of your claims invalid and issue an order that your patent is invalid or unenforceable. Your ability to fully use your IP quickly goes to zero.

Table 5. Comparison of Property Rights: Intellectual (IP), Real (RP), Personal (PP).

RP and PP	Patent (IP)
Can sell	Same
Can assign	Same
Can license	Same
Can cross license	Same
Can trade	Same
Can donate	Same
Unlimited ownership time	Patents expire after 20 yrs
Only one party can own	More than one party can claim
No change in scope	Court can declare patent invalid

Disposing of Patent Rights

If the owner does not want to retain all patent rights to be able to exclude others, the usual ways of disposing of the patent rights are as follows:

- Selling
- Licensing
  Exclusive
  Non-exclusive
  With a reserved right
  With a field of use restriction
  Cross licensing
- Donating – To a non-profit organization, such as a university, can be a big tax deduction for the patent owner.

Commercializing Claims as Most Usual Disposal

If you do not use a patent to protect a product, composition or process of yours, the most common way to commercialize the claimed subject matter is by licensing. Royalties vary considerably depending on the industry, subject matter involved, the amount of exclusivity involved as well as the perceived strength/validity of the patent.

With some subject matter, licensees are not interested unless they are the exclusive licensee because they do not want to put substantial resources into development and sales only to then face major competition. The pharmaceutical industry is a good example of this.

With other subject matter, the licensee only wants freedom to use the patent subject matter. A good example of this is the Cohen Boyer patent where hundreds, if not thousands, of licenses were granted.

II.
FREEDOM TO OPERATE

What Is Freedom to Operate?

Freedom to operate means all of the following:

- Your product/composition will not infringe any unexpired patents,

- The process used to manufacture your product/composition does not infringe any unexpired patents, and

- The name of your product does not infringe any Trademark,

- You possess any regulatory certificates required by the Federal Drug Administration (FDA),

- You possess any regulatory approvals to operate because of environmental issues (whether state or federal).

In summary, you will not infringe any patent in making or selling your invention and you possess all regulatory approvals required to make and sell your invention. You are "Free to Operate."

The latter part of Preface meant to show that a patent does not give the owner/assignee the right to use the claimed invention, only the right to exclude others. So the reason to obtain patents is to exclude others.

In theory you do not need a patent to begin to market a new product. You do need to make sure you are not infringing any patent or trademark and have any necessary regulatory/environmental permits that are required. I used the term "in theory" because as a matter of law, you do not need a patent to begin to market a new product or composition or use a new process; you just have to make sure you are not infringing a third party's patent. But assume you are not infringing any third-party patent and develop a bell ringer of a product (without patent protection). What is going to happen?

Large corporations will learn of your success, copy your product and, using their vast resources, maybe have it made in overseas facilities (where they can have it made in bulk for less than you can) and then sell it at their cost. They can afford to break-even or even take a loss for a period of time to gain market share and push you out of the business you started. Once you have left the playing arena, they are free to up their price because the competition you brought to the marketplace is gone. If you had a patent, you could exclude them from the market and be the sole vendor. If they willfully infringe to challenge you, you can get up to triple your damages and your attorney fees paid.

Being unaware of a patent does not mean you will not infringe. Even if you were totally unaware of a patent that you are infringing upon, the owner can still get an injunction stopping you from making, using and/or selling and have a court order you to pay the patent owner any damage he/

she incurred. The patentee's[12] damages may well be more than your profits. This is the case even if you searched for any patents you might infringe and missed it for some reason.

However, in the real world, if you have very little in sales and agree to stop infringing, it is quite common for the patent owner to not file an infringement action and not seek damages. What the patentee really wants is the exclusive right to market, and if you agree to stop selling that right is assured.

Willful Infringement

"Willful infringement" is a totally different. If you are aware of a patent, knowingly infringe upon it and are caught, 35 U.S.C. §284 provides the court can increase the actual damages up to triple and §285 provides that you can be required to pay the patentee's attorney fees. Willful infringement can get very expensive very fast.

At one time I represented Asgrow Seed Company where farmers were illegally selling Asgrow's Plant Variety Protection Act (PVPA) soybeans. The PVPA is very similar to the patent statute for our purposes of discussing willful infringement. In an Arkansas case the defendant was knowingly selling Asgrow's product. When I had our agent make a buy of the protected soybeans to show an infringing sale was made, I made sure our agent was wired to record the conversation.

The purchaser asked for the product by name, Asgrow's A1234 but the seller put "Arkansas blend" on the invoice. The purchaser said, "My

---

[12] The patentee often assigns his/her rights to his/her employer (the assignee) or gives them to a licensee in a license agreement. Rather than repeating "patentee/ assignee/licensee" each time, I will just use the term "patentee." Understand that it includes either assignee or licensee in the appropriate situations.

boss does not want Arkansas blend. He told me specifically to get Asgrow A1234." The seller then replied, "This is A1234, but I am not supposed to be selling them so I put Arkansas Blend on the invoice." That was excellent evidence of willful infringement. In a deposition, the seller—not knowing he had been recorded—stated that he did not know he was not supposed to be selling A1234 as seed. Add perjury to the list of the infringer's problems.

The defendant's evidence indicated that he was making about $1 profit per item bag of seed sold. Asgrow made about $4/bag profit and therefore was losing that amount for each bag the defendant sold. The judge doubled the damages and added attorney's fees (about $1/unit). So it cost the defendant about $9/bag he sold when his profit was only about $1/bag. He had to sell part of his farm to pay the judgment.

A Freedom to Operate Opinion (FTOO)

A FTOO is a legal opinion that a patent attorney issues for a client after performing an infringement search of the relevant patents, comparing the claims of the patents which claim similar subject matter with the client's product/composition/ process and deciding whether or not there is literal infringement. If not, then the attorney determines whether or not there is infringement under the Doctrine of Equivalents by examining the prosecution history of relevant patents and evaluating the validity of the patents with claims which "read on"[13] his client's product/composition/ process.

---

[13] "Read on" is a term of art that patent attorneys use to mean, "includes or covers."

The Doctrine of Equivalents (DOE)

The DOE is an equitable doctrine which permits a judge to find infringement of a claim even though there is no literal infringement. Even though there is no literal infringement, a judge can find infringement under the DOE if in the judge's opinion it is the equitable thing to do.

Some judges use the DOE when a third party is able to use the claimed invention without literally infringing by stepping just outside the wording of the claim and, in the judge's opinion, it is unfair to the patentee to permit a third party to in essence steal the invention. This is usually found if the third party is doing the same thing in the same way to get the same result.

The judge also determines what elements are in the claim and what elements the third party is using. Do you infringe if a patent claim reads as any of these below:

(a) "A process .... in the temperature[14] range of 0–100°," and you use 101°?

(b) "A process .... in the temperature range of 0–100°," and you use 102°?

(c) "A process .... in the temperature range of 0–100°," and you use 103°?

(d) "A process .... in the temperature range of 0–100°," and you use 104°?

(e) "A process .... in the temperature range of 0–100°," and you use 110°?

(f) "A process .... in the temperature range of 0–100°," and you use 115°? or

(x) "A hammer with a handle of oak, cherry or maple," and you use a walnut handle?

In (a) through (f) and (x), there is no literal infringement. However, there could be

---

[14] All temperatures are given in degrees Celsius.

infringement under the equitable Doctrine of Equivalents. DOE cases usually divide into two distinct groups, depending on the judicial philosophy of the particular judge and how he/she applies the law.

One group is comprised of judges who state that they are not going to permit a third party to steal the patented invention by just stepping over the line, from 100° to 101° or 102°. However, at some point (perhaps at 110° or 115°), the same judge will say that is too far from the line and find the use not infringing.

Another judicial philosophy follows the reasoning that the patentee had competent scientists, experienced patent attorneys and if the patentee wanted 101° or 103° or 105° or 110° or even 150°, the patentee could have claimed it, but did not. These judges believe that third parties need to know from the wording of the claims what property belongs to the patentees and what does not. Third parties need to know when they will and will not infringe so as to be able to conduct their business. The patentee had the opportunity to word the claim as the patentee chose, and the patentee is stuck with it. If these judges grant any equivalents, it is usually very minimal.

Hence, claim interpretation is not straight forward and a reason one needs a patent attorney for a FTOO.

Why Obtain a Freedom to Operate Opinion?

If you are concerned that your product, composition or process *might* infringe upon a patent you are aware of, you should get a patent attorney to give you an FTOO. The reason is, even if you don't think you infringe and/or you believe the patent to be invalid, it still will be willful infringement if you are sued and if the trier of fact finds that you indeed did infringe and the patent is valid. That could subject you to triple damages and payment of the other party's attorney fees.

You probably can insulate yourself from these enhanced damages by obtaining an FTOO. If the opinion is done after a thorough search, a studied evaluation of the claims and your product, composition or process and well-reasoned assessment of validity for the FTOO to conclude that (1) your product, composition or process does not infringe any independent claim of any unexpired patent and/or (2) if it does infringe, the patent(s) are invalid. The judge is then likely to conclude that you had a good faith belief (even though that belief was wrong) that you were not infringing and/or the patent was invalid. Therefore, the judge will not increase your damages or require payment of the other party's attorney fees.

An FTOO is just that: *a legal opinion*; it could be wrong. It is a legal opinion and not a business decision. If the FTOO finds you might or will infringe and the patent is probably valid, that is very important information you should have before making the business decision as to discontinue the product, composition or process, seek a license or gamble and move ahead.

A word of caution: Too often small businesses focus on saving funds and avoid getting an FTOO opinion from a patent attorney. They ask their general attorney to just write them a letter that they are not infringing or the patent in question is invalid. Judges are well aware that clients often buy opinions, especially from attorneys not qualified to issue such an opinion or that the attorney did not go through the steps and analysis required as evidenced by the quality of the opinion issued. Don't cut corners here; do it right. If your product, composition or process is possibly/probably claimed by a patent, find a patent attorney and request an FTOO.

Having an FTOO opinion does not guarantee that, should you be found to infringe and the patent is valid, you will not be required to pay increased damages or the other party's attorney fees. The Judge's determination is likely to turn on the quality of the FTOO.

The first step in doing an FTOO is to do an "infringement search." An infringement search is searching for U.S. patents that claim subject matter likely to include your invention or what you want to do. Patents claiming similar subject matter will be classified (class/subclass) the same. The first step is something you can do; the second step is something you cannot do.

Once these likely and/or similar patents are found, the second step is to determine if your product, composition or process falls within the scope of any of the independent claims of these patents. You can make a preliminary determination of whether or not your product, composition or process falls within the scope of the independent claims by dividing the patents into two groups. The first group includes those patents whose subject matter is so far different from yours that they need not be reviewed by a patent attorney. The second group is comprised of those which are similar or close; for anything that is close, the final determination needs to be made by a patent attorney.

Conducting An Infringement Search

Proceed by acknowledging difficulty and uncertainty.

Discussion which follows is limited to U.S. jurisdiction only. One can only infringe a patent in the relevant jurisdiction. If you are concerned about selling a product in Germany or South Korea, you will need to do an infringement search in those countries. A "quick and dirty" way to get some idea of whether or not there is a patent in one of those countries is to do the U.S. infringement search and then, if you find a patent that is highly relevant, your patent attorney can quickly find if any foreign equivalent. However, the converse is not true. If you don't find a U.S. patent that is relevant, that does not mean a foreign patent is not relevant. In Chapter III, under the statutory requirement for Novelty, you will see that Syntex had a patent on a topical steroid formulation in Great Britain, but not one in the Untied States.

With regard to a product or composition, either is just one item in your search. However, even if there are no patents claiming your product or composition, you still need to be sure that you are not infringing any patents in the production (process) of making your product/composition.

Process is more complicated. If a process has seven steps, realize that six intermediate items stand between the starting material and the product; each of these intermediates has to be searched, as well as the seven process steps.

If you have a widget X that you want to sell in the U.S. and you would like to check whether there are any patents you might infringe upon, you need to do take these two steps:

1. Determine what class/subclass the widget X would be classified in, if you were to patent it;

2. Examine the independent claims of all unexpired patents in that class/subclass comparing the elements of the claim to widget X.

Even if widget X does not meet all the elements of a claim exactly, infringement under the Doctrine of Equivalents could still exist. That is another reason a patent attorney needs to make the final determination.

The first problem is most difficult: how do you determine what class and subclass in which widget X would be classified if it were to be patented? The search, and ultimately FTOO, is only as good as the classification because if you are looking in the wrong class/subclass, you may never find a patent you could be infringing.

Theoretically, I know four ways to find the class/subclass:

1. Use the USPTO Manual of Patent Classification, *see http://www.uspto.gov/web/patents/ classification/selectnumwithtitle.htm;*

2. Try to get the assistance of a patent examiner in the Art Group handling similar subject matter;

3. Retain the services of a professional who does searching and has experience in classification. I use a former patent examiner who charges $150 to classify an item. He verifies his decision with current patent examiners.

4. Go about it indirectly yourself.

With regard to the first of these four (above) even after 35 years of patent practice, it takes an immense amount of time and I am not always certain I have the correct class/subclass. You will be able to eliminate most classes and reduce your options to a few possibilities and that is very helpful. To do the second you need to be in Washington, DC, and go to the USPTO. Even if you do, good luck trying to get someone to help you. A fast and realistic way is the third of four, but know that professionals can be wrong. On more than one occasion when dealing with very valuable commercial products, I had two different searchers tell me where they would classify a chemical compound. Most often they supply you with the one they think is most likely, but also two or three others. While some classes/subclasses were the same for both searchers, usually they each included some classes/subclasses that the other did not. To be safe I searched all of them.

The method I recommend for a number of reasons is the fourth. As you go through this, you will learn an incredible amount of information about similar products, compositions or processes. The good news, it is free; the bad news, it is very time consuming (but rewarding). One client searched through almost a thousand patents to find three very relevant ones.

The process for doing #4 is to do a key word search of all USPTO patents. When you find a number of patents of interest, make a list of their class/subclasses. When you have a good number of them, you will begin to notice a pattern of the patents with the most similar subject matter having the same class/subclass or being cross-referenced in the same class/subclass. When you are convinced that you have located the correct class/subclass because all the most relevant patents are in the same place, you have found it! If not all patents, but most of them are there, then collect enough information to identify a second or even a third possibility. It is more work to search more than one class/subclass, but it increases the probability that you have the correct class/subclass and will find any patents that claim your invention.

Twelve major steps comprise my recommended indirect method:

I. Go to *http://patft.uspto.gov/*
   • On the left side under PatFT: Patents, click on Quick Search
   • On the next page, in the box marked "Term 1:" put a key word in the box marked "Field 1:"
   • Leave "All Fields" as is.
   • Hit search.

A list of all patents contain your "key word" will appear. Review the titles for anything relevant to your product, composition or process. If the title gives it a chance to be relevant, open the document and go to the claims. Check *only* the independent claims. Is what is being claimed at all close or relevant to your invention, product, composition or process? If not, go on to the next one; if it is relevant, go to step II.

II. The front page of each U.S. Patent has a meaningful code number, *e.g.,* "[52] U.S. Cl. **123/456.**" This is the class and subclass for this patent expressed as 123/456. Following the bold number may be a series of similar numbers. These are cross references for this patent, meaning similar subject matter class and subclass. Record the patent number and class/subclass.

III. Repeat this procedure, using a fairly large number of key words and checking the patents that come up.

IV. Record the class/subclass for the most relevant patents and also the cross-reference class/subclasses.

V. After a period of time you will find with the patents that are most similar to your invention a pattern will develop; the class/subclasses will begin to repeat to one or a few.

VI. The class/subclass designations that most often repeat for the most relevant patents are the probably the correct class/subclass for your invention. If this invention was previously patented by a third party, this is where it will likely be found. Use these class/subclass numbers for steps VII–XII which follow.

VII. On the Internet, go to the USPTO Full-Text Data base to search for your desired class/subclass as follows:
- Go to *http://patft.uspto.gov/*
- On the left side under PatFT: Patents, click on Quick Search.
- In the box marked Term 1:, put the class and subclass you want to search separated by a "/"; for example (34/60).
- In the box marked Field 1:, put "Current US Classification."
- Do not do anything with Term 2: and Field 2:.
- Hit search.

VIII. Go back and find the patents that were filed about 21 years ago and then work your way to the present.

IX. If you can definitely eliminate a patent by its title, do so.

X. If not eliminated, open the patent and go to the claims.

XI. Examine **each and every *independent* claim** to see if your invention is contained in the claim, *i.e.,* the wording of the claim encompasses your invention. Even if not exact, but close, record the patent number. Skip *all* dependent claims.

XII. Do steps VII–XI for each class/subclass.

Give all the patent numbers that you recorded as including your invention, or close to it, to your attorney to evaluate (with your assistance). Even though your infringement search is complete, you still most likely need an infringement opinion as to whether or not you have freedom to operate. If you find nothing close to your invention, it is a business decision to take the risk of moving forward without seeking an FTOO.

Remember, even if you do not find any patents claiming subject matter close to your product or composition, it is possible that you could infringe patents in the process of making your product or composition. In the introductory example of Tipranavir, the assignee had not one but two patents claiming the product which did not infringe any third-party patents, but the process to make it did. Therefore, without a license to the patent claiming the intermediate necessary for production of the product, the assignee would not have been able to market the product. While that is a chemical patent, it is possible to infringe processes to make electrical or mechanical subject matter.

How Do Infringement Searches Differ from Patentability Searches?

In essence these searches are about the same as the difference between Albert Einstein and Marilyn Monroe! An infringement search is very narrow; a patentability search is as broad as is possible (*see* Table 6).

While doing an infringement search, one searches:

- Only United States patents;
- Only the relevant classes/subclasses;
- Only back about 20 years and
- Only the independent claims.

For a patentability search, one searches:

- Not only U.S. patents, but patents in all countries;

- Not only the relevant classes/subclasses, but all classes/subclasses that disclose any relevant information;

- Not back just 20 years, but back to Adam and Eve;

- Not just the independent claims, but the entire specification;

- Not only patents, but journals, newspapers, trade journals, magazines, thesis, scientific publications, commercial advertisements, etc., etc. and

- Not just in English, but in all languages world wide.

Table 6. Comparison of Search Types.

Specifics	Infringement	Patentability
Jurisdiction	United States only	All countries
Documents	Patents	Patents, scientific journals, theses, trade publications, commercial ads, etc.
Patents	Independent claims	Claims and specification
Language	English	All languages
Time	Only back 20 years	No time limit

In summary, infringement searches are very narrow and limited, while patentability searches are totally open-ended because all types of information can be "prior art" to patentability.

Be Very Careful With Search Terms

With an infringement search, one only needs to search the USPTO data base which is available to the public. However, when doing a broader search for patentability, not all data bases are available to the public.

An M.D., Ph.D. gynecologist was a Corporate VP in a pharmaceutical company and had many patents as a physician-scientist before becoming part of the administration. He performed his own patentability searches. His invention was the use of subcutaneous (SQ) administration of the female hormones estrogens (estrone, estradiol, estratriol, PREMARIN Tablets, etc.) and progestogens (progesterone, PROVERA Tablets, etc.) to treat menopause, endometriosis and contraception.

When he told me of his invention, I asked him why he thought it would be patentable (nonobvious), in view of intramuscular (IM) administration of the same pharmaceutical agents for the same exact uses. He replied that IM worked well because there was plenty of blood flow there to absorb the pharmaceutical agents and then distribute them throughout the body. However, the prior art taught there was not enough blood flow under the skin for the pharmaceutical agents such as these lipophilic substances to be absorbed. Further, he had conducted both infringement and patentability searches and all the documents taught away from his invention, *i.e.,* that it should not work. However, when he tried administering the pharmaceutical agents SQ, indeed it did work.

I informed him that his was the exact type of evidence we needed to prove nonobviousness and obtain a patent. Because he had already had done both searches and was a very experienced scientist, I filed a patent application that claimed a method of treating menopause, endometriosis and contraception by administration of SQ estrogens

and progestogens. The first Office Action I received
on the merits was a rejection of all claims because
the subject matter was not novel, but known.
The Examiner cited U.S. Patents 5,753,639 and
5,814,340; I could not believe it because, if the
Examiner was correct, the inventor has missed
these documents. So I quickly obtained copies
of these patents and compiled Table 7 (below) to
compare the SQ invention and the two prior art
patents:

Table 7. Claimed Invention Compared to Patents Granted.			
Document	**Admin**	**Utility**	**Pharm Agents**
patent application	SQ	Menopause Endometriosis Contraception	Estrogens Progestogens
5,753,639 5,814,340	SQ	Menopause Endometriosis Contraception	Anti-androgens

Both the route of administration and the utilities
were identical. With regard to the pharmaceutical
agents, the two patents did not refer to the two
female hormones as female hormones or by their
chemical or generic or trademark names. They
used the term "anti-androgens" to mean female
hormones. Androgens are male hormones. So
they referred to the female hormones as anti-male
hormones.

In patent law there is an axiom that patent
attorneys can be their own lexicographers. Female
hormones are considered by many to be the
opposite of male hormones, so anti-androgen was
not totally unreasonable even though very few
would use that terminology. The problem here was
the physician used all sorts of common terms to
include the female hormones in his searches, but
never thought to call them anti-androgens. I too

would never have thought of that and would have missed the two patents as he did.

Searcher beware! Choice of terms is crucial to success.

In doing a patentability search, one needs to include subject matter in foreign countries in foreign languages. The problem is one of translation of terms. For example, in China if you search for the term "giraffe" you will find there is no such animal. Yet if you showed a picture of a giraffe to someone from China, they will nod and inform you it is not a giraffe at all but rather a deer with a long neck. If you then search for the term "zebra" again you will find there is no such animal. Then if you searched for striped deer or deer with stripes, again you will find there is no such animal. However, if you tried striped horse you will find what we in the U.S. call a zebra.

If you find a number of relevant documents, you know they exist and you have found them. If you don't find anything, you are not sure whether the situation is (a) nothing relevant exists or (b) they exist but you have not found them.

Be very careful in your searching.

If you are not experienced, it may well pay to retain someone who does searching as a full-time occupation.

III.
GETTING U.S. PATENTS

Statutory Requirements for Patentability

The patent statute, 35 U.S.C. §§, has many requirements for patentability but Table 8 lists most important ones you need to know. Let your patent attorney attend to the rest.

Table 8. Relevant Sections of the Patent Statute.	
35 U.S.C.	**Subject Matter**
§ 101	Utility
§ 102	Novelty
§ 103	Obviousness
§ 112, pp 1	Written Description
§ 112, pp 1	Teach one skilled in the art "how to make"
§ 112, pp 1	Teach one skilled in the art "how to use"
§ 112, pp 1	Best Mode
§ 112, pp 2	Particularly point out & distinctly claiming

The "Written Description" and the §112 pp 2 requirement are solely for the attorney, with nothing for the non-attorney. With rare exception an inventor can readily teach one skilled in the arts of "How To Make and Use" the invention.

Disclosure of the "Best Mode" just means not trying to hide the preferred materials, steps, conditions, etc. These requirements are relatively easy to comply with and generally should not, and do not, prevent obtaining a patent.

That just leaves the first three requirements. I have had only one invention report in which the invention did not have utility; lack of utility is very rarely an issue. If the invention lacks utility, why would anyone care if you have a patent on it?

§101 UTILITY

In drafting and prosecuting about 300 patent applications over 30 years I have only had one invention which did not have statutory utility.

The invention was a very potent compound for inhibiting cancer in a cell-free system. Its inventor filed an invention report with his employer. The problem was that while he could inhibit cancer replication in cell-free situations, he could not get the compound in the cell. Unless he could find a way to get the compound into a mammalian cell, the compound had no commercial utility, only research utility. The problem the inventor needed to solve was how to get the compound of interest into cells.

One does not need to know *how* or *why* something works. The patent statute does not require you to explain how or why the invention works. For example, if the invention is a new antibiotic, the inventor needs to allege that it is useful as an antibiotic, but is not required to explain how or why it works.

Further, to be useful a pharmaceutical need not *cure* cancer; *treating* cancer is sufficient. Actually if you alleged it cured cancer, the patent examiner probably would challenge that. Whereas if you allege that it treats (slows, prevents other effects, etc.) cancer, that utility should be accepted.

I firmly believe that you need to comply with all the requirements of the statute, but I also firmly believe the inventor should not submit information that is not required.

§102 NOVELTY

Novelty can be an issue, but it is rare. Novelty has procedural and substantive aspects.

Procedural Aspect

Procedurally you can lose patentable subject matter by actions *you* commit prior to the filing of a (provisional) patent application. Basically §102(b) provides you shall be entitled to a patent unless you described the invention in a printed publication anywhere or had it in public use or on sale in the U.S. more than one year prior to filing of a (provisional) patent application. This one-year grace period is unique to the U.S.; foreign countries require absolute novelty. So if you want global patent coverage (which most businesses do), *do not* do any of the above until after the filing of a (provisional) patent application.

Under §102(c) you can lose your invention if you abandon it.

Under §102(d) you can lose patent rights if you patent the subject matter of your invention in a foreign country more than a year before filing here. Very few U.S. inventors or business file in foreign countries prior to filing here so this very rarely is of concern.

Quite often inventors and small business have an "invention" for which they want to file a patent application to obtain a patent and ultimately sell their product or use their process commercially. However, both the inventor and small business are almost always short funded. They wish to disclose their "invention" to third parties for both business advice in moving forward and to seek funding. This is done all the time without violating the absolute novelty bar by using a Confidential Disclosure Agreement (CDA).

CDAs are simple one-page agreements in which you agree to disclose confidential information to a third party (public) for a specific purpose and they agree to keep it secret for some reasonable period of time. The agreement provides that if the third party can prove that they had the information legally prior to your disclosure to them, or they acquire it legally from some party who has the right to disclose it to them, they are free to use it regardless of the CDA. Business uses these agreements all the time to disclose confidential (patentable subject) matter without making it public and violating the absolutely novelty bar requirement. Any patent attorney can help you with a CDA.

Substantive Aspect
Novelty is a very, very fine line and usually not too difficult to obtain. You cannot patent that which is known; all else is novel or new.

Novelty (§102) is often confused with "obviousness" (§103) by non-patent attorneys with disastrous effects. You need to keep these legal issues separate. At this point all you should be concerned with is, "is your invention NEW?" An unfortunate happening will exemplify how a number of very experienced, excellent scientists—all of whom were thought leaders in the world—missed a patentable invention (and millions in royalties) by combining "novelty" with "obviousness" in their minds to mean "unpatentable."

Years ago women were treated for menopause with estrogens alone by taking a tablet of estrogen daily. A deleterious side effect was endometrial hyperplasia which is a significant risk factor for the development or even co-existence of endometrial cancer.

By adding about 15 days of progesterone a month, the side effects of the estrogen were eliminated. However, when the women finished the 15 days of progesterone each month, they had a period. The vast majority of these menopausal women did not want to experience periods again and stopped taking the menopausal therapy.

At an OB-GYN convention in London, the convention delegates and wives went on a Thames River boat trip. A Toronto M.D., Dr. Plunkett, met Professor Whitehead of Kings College and asked him how to solve the problem of women having periods again when 15 days of progesterone was added to the continuous estrogen. Professor Whitehead replied, "Just make the progesterone continuous and uninterrupted like the estrogen." So Dr. Plunkett returned to Toronto and filed a patent application claiming low-dose, continuous, combined estrogen–progesterone for treating menopause. He was granted U.S. Patent 4,826,831 in May 1989.

My client had a leading progesterone product on the market and was very familiar with the leading researchers in the area. Because of the information exchanged by these leading researchers, my client was convinced that the continuous combined low-dose estrogen–progesterone treatment claimed in the Plunkett patent had been used many times prior to Plunkett's filing. Therefore, the Plunkett patent was invalid because 35 U.S.C. §102(a) provides,

"A person shall be entitled to a patent unless—

(a) the invention was known or used
by others in this country. . . before the
invention thereof by the applicant for
patent, . . ."

My client requested I contact these researchers
to see if they had previously used the low-dose
combination in the U.S. prior to Plunkett's filing
date. If so, I was to collect the evidence I needed to
invalidate Plunkett's patent.

Being researchers and consultants with the
pharmaceutical industry, they all were very
familiar with patents and many had patents in
their own name. The researchers I contacted
included a UCLA professor, a Case Western
professor, the president of the International
Menopause Society (who practiced in Florida), a
Harvard professor, another professor from Boston,
a private physician in NY and a few others.
Besides those in the U.S., for other reasons, I
contacted Dr. Whitehead, another professor at
Kings College and a professor in Malmo, Sweden.
All had used a continuous, combined, low-dose
estrogen–progesterone combination to treat
menopause before Plunkett had filed his patent
application.

After I collected the information I was seeking from
each, I asked each one, "Why didn't you patent
this treatment?" The answers were identical, "I
didn't think it was patentable." Patentability is not
a statutory requirement; novelty and obviousness
are. They were combining the two in their minds
and thought it was either not novel because
they and others had used (but not publicly) or,
if novel, it was obvious. I learned most likely it
was the later because they all knew, and most
practiced, giving continuous progesterone to
female athletes, politicians and others who did not
want to have periods at inopportune times such as
honeymoons.

Plunkett licensed his patent to Wyeth-Ayerst who sold PREMPRO tablets covered by the patent. It was a billion dollar seller. With just a two percent royalty, the licensor would get $20,000,000 in annual royalties.

Following is an example of a better outcome when you keep "novelty" and "obviousness" separate, and not prejudge about patentability.

When I finished law school and took my first job, I had absolutely no experience with patents. I was given a patent application to practice with that had already been written, filed and rejected by the USPTO under 35 U.S.C. §102(b) for lack of novelty. They told me not to worry if I could not obtain a patent because it appeared the claimed subject matter was not patentable (had already been rejected). If the researchers in the Plunkett situation had followed the approach below, they would have been the patentee enjoying the royalties, not Plunkett.

The patent application I received had only one claim and that was to only one compound, diflorasone diacetate[15] (Figure 3):

**Figure 3. Claim for Structural Formula
of Diflorasone Diacetate.**

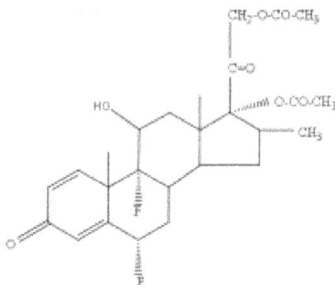

---

[15] Diflorasone diacetate is 6α,9α-difluoro-11β,17α,21-trihydroxy-16β-methylpregna-1,4-diene,3,20-dione 17,21-diacetate. It is still on the market as FLORONE Cream or Ointment.

The prior art was a patent to Syntex which claimed a compound of the formula shown in Figure 4:

Figure 4. Prior Art for Structural Formula Granted to Syntex.

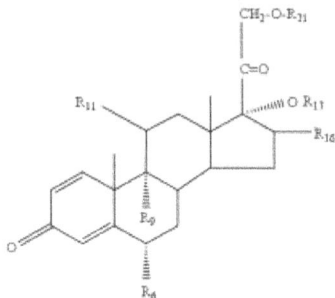

The R_6, R_9, R_{11}, ... R_{21} variable substituents were defined broadly enough to include the atoms and groups at the designated positions of diflorasone diacetate. Hence, diflorasone diacetate was within the scope of the Syntex patent.

The law is that even if a compound is within the generic scope of the prior art it is still novel, if the prior art does not specifically mention or exemplify it. Other compounds were exemplified and specifically mentioned by Syntex; diflorasone diacetate was not. When I pointed this out to the Examiner, he withdrew the rejection for lack of novelty, but added a rejection under 35 U.S.C. §103 for obviousness since the claimed compound was so similar to known compounds. That was a correct rejection to make.

Next I tried to find something different about this compound compared to the prior art to overcome the rejection. Structurally the compound is very similar to other steroids used topically for anti-inflammatory purposes. I contacted the inventor in an effort to try and find something "surprising and unexpected" to overcome the obviousness rejection.

Initially the inventor, Dr. Carl Schlagel, said there was nothing really unusual about the claimed compound. When I followed up by asking whether there wasn't anything that surprised him about this compound, he responded, "There is one thing that surprised me." I then asked, "What was that?" and he replied, "Virtually all topical anti-inflammatory steroids can be used either with or without occlusion[16] but this one can be used both ways."

So I filed a declaration with Dr. Schlagel's testimony and his conclusion that, as an experienced scientist with topical anti-inflammatory steroids, it was surprising and unexpected to him that this compound could be used both with and without occlusion. I then made the argument that since this compound had surprising and unexpected properties, as evidenced by Dr. Schlagel's testimony, the compound was nonobvious under §103. The Examiner agreed, withdrew the rejection and allowed the claim. Victory! Diflorasone diacetate was patentable.

During the process above, I separated novelty (§102) and obviousness (§103) and, since I was able to show the compound was both novel and nonobvious, I obtained a patent. This is what you need to do with your inventions; do not look to the end result as patentability. Rather see if you can meet each of the statutory requirements. If you can, you should obtain your patent.

The best way for me to teach you how you can best estimate the chances your invention is obvious/nonobivous is by a short statement of the law and then examples. It is my experience that the examples are the best teachers and also best remembered.

---

[16] An occlusion means "with a covering" like plastic wrap to keep moisture in.

Novelty can be divided into two types for discussion:

Type 1. ANYTHING, ANYTHING that is new, no matter how close to something known is novel.

Type 2. Anything inside the scope of what is known but what is not (a) specifically described or (b) exemplified, is novel as long as the broader disclosure is such that each member is not readily apparent. These are termed "selection inventions" because they are selected from previous invention.

Things that exemplify Type 1 are (a) Known, *e.g.*, a chair with four legs and (b) Novel, *e.g.*, a chair with five legs, as close as can be, but if there are no chairs known with five legs, it is novel. If a chair with five legs is Known (•), then Novel (») would be a chair with six legs, as close as can be, but if there are no chairs known with six legs, it is novel.

Novelty applies to technical subject matter listed previously on page 3. Type 1 chemical examples that include the compounds estrogen–progestogen, vitamin D and an AIDS pharmaceutical:

The Plunkett example
• Known, using estrogen continuously + 15 days of progestogen for menopause.
» Novel, using estrogen continuously + 30/31 days of progestogen for menopause, s*ee* U.S. Patent 4,826,831.

Vitamin D
• Known, 25 hydroxy cocalciferol (25-HCC) is claimed in U.S. Patent 3,565,924.
» Novel, 25-HCC hemihydrate is novel and is claimed in U.S. Patent 3,833,622. 25-HCC is a semi-solid which is difficult to formulate. 25-HCC hemihydrate is a free

flowing crystalline solid which is surprising and unexpected (nonobvious) and therefore patentable, see U.S. Patent 3,833,622.

AIDS pharmaceutical:
* Known, delavirdine mesylate in crystal form (form D).
» Novel, delavirdine mesylate in crystal form (forms S and T). Crystal form D is hydroscopic (picks up water from the air), whereas crystal forms S and T are not hydroscopic which is surprising and unexpected (nonobvious). Therefore, forms S and T are patentable, see U.S. Patent 6,452,007 B1.

Process examples can deal with chemical reactions and important human physiology.
* Known, a process to produce a formula X compound comprised of reacting a compound of formula A with a compound of formula B at a temperature of 20°–100°.
» Novel, a process to produce a compound of formula X comprised of reacting a compound of formula A with a compound of formula B at a temperature of 101°.
* Known, use minoxidil to treat hypertension.
» Novel, use minoxidil to grow hair, see U.S. Patents 4,139,619 and 4,596,812.
* Known, use tirilazad to treat head injury and stroke.
» Novel, use tirilazad for ophthalmic use, see U.S. Patent 5,124,154.
» Novel, use tirilazad for preventing surgical adhesions, see WO96/15795.

Mechanical and electrical device examples of Type 1 Novelty are:
* Known, hammers with oak, cherry, maple handles.
» Novel, hammer with walnut handle.

- Known, a digital computer chip with a capacity of 2,500,000 units.
» Novel, a digital computer chip with a capacity of 2,600,00 units.

I am not saying these inventions are patentable; they may well be obvious under §103, but they are novel. One step at a time.

It is well known that small changes can be very important and valuable and novel. This is especially true with a small change in a process, particularly in the cracking of petroleum. The USPTO recognizes this, and its term for process claims where the improvement is very small are called Jepson claims. They acknowledge the process is similar to the prior art by the preamble, "An improved process. . . " and conclude by identifying the improvement, ". . . where the improvement comprises. . . ." The chemical process above written in Jepson format is:

> An improved process for the production of a compound of formula X which comprised reacting a compound of formula A with a compound of formula B where the improvement comprises performing the reaction at a temperature of 101°.

Examples of things that fall under Type 2 Novelty include compounds.

- Known, a process to produce a compound of formula X comprised of reacting a compound of formula A with a compound of formula B at a temperature of 20°–100°. Assume there is a preferred range of 30°–50° with examples at 21, 30, 32, 33, 36, 40, 45, 50, 60, 80 and 93°.
» Novel, a process to produce a compound of formula X comprised of reacting a compound of formula A with a compound of formula B at a temperature of 65°–72°. The 65°–72° range is within the previous invention, but it was not

described nor exemplified so it is novel and can be the subject matter of another invention.

An actual example is:

» Known – **Figure 5. Bicyclic-Heterocyclic Amines,** *see* U.S. Patent 5,502,187.

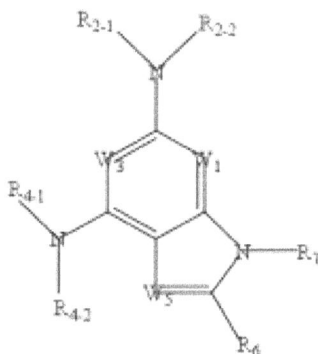

» Novel – **Figure 6. Pyrimido[4,5-b]indoles,** *see* U.S. Patent 5,795,986.

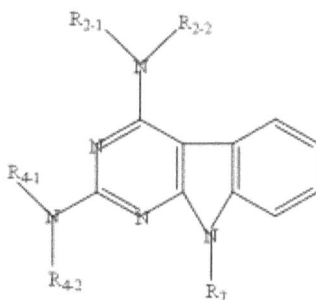

Pyrimido[4,5-b]indoles are within the scope of bicyclic-heterocyclic amines; they are a special type. Since they were not specifically described nor exemplified in the 187 patent, they were novel. Because pyrimido[4,5-b]indoles had surprising and unexpected properties not taught by the 187 patent, they were not obvious and therefore patentable.

» Novel – **Figure 7. Bis-1-pyrrolidinyl indoles,** *see* U.S. Patent 5,932,728.

Bis-1-pyrrolidinyl indoles are within the scope of pyrimido[4,5-b]indoles, where both amino groups are pyrrolidinyl. Because the bis-1-pyrrolidinyl indoles had surprising and unexpected properties not taught by the 986 patent, they were not obvious and therefore patentable.

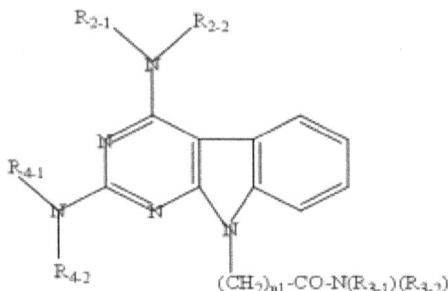

This is a very unusual situation of a selection invention within a selection invention. This is the only time I have ever done that. It very well illustrates how one can have an invention within the scope of another invention, Type 2.

§103 OBVIOUSNESS

In most instances if there is a problem in obtaining a patent, it is here, with the issue requirement of nonobviousness. The equivalent term in most foreign countries is "inventive step." If an invention lacks "inventive step," it is not patentable.

The issue and fight for patentability in the vast majority of situations is over the issue of whether the claimed subject matter is "obvious" to one of ordinary skill in the art. Hence, in deciding whether to file a patent application on an "invention," the most important analysis is usually whether the invention is "obvious" within the meaning of §103. Most of the information in this section relates to this issue.

The patent examiner will ask the two fundamental questions, (1) What does the prior art teach one skilled in the art about the invention? and (2) What is surprising and unexpected about the claimed invention in view of the prior art?

Surprising and unexpected properties/results/ effects are the factual basis for the legal conclusion of nonobviousness. Better or superior is not nonobvious (◊), if it is predictable from the prior art.

Assuming a five-legged chair is "novel," it is certainly "useful." You can easily "teach one skilled in the art how to make and how to use it." So the only statutory requirement left is §103, obviousness. While novel, what is surprising and unexpected about a five-legged chair? Nothing. So it is obvious and unpatentable.

The best way to understand how patent examiners will apply this statutory requirement is to see how it has been applied in the past:

• Known–Minoxidil is useful to treat hypertension.
» Novel–Minoxidil is useful to grow hair.
◊ Nonobvious–No teaching in the prior art that minoxidil will grow hair.

• Known—Rubradirin in useful to treat staph infections.
» Novel—Rubradirin is useful to treat methicillin resistant staph.
◊ Nonobvious–No teaching in the prior art that Rubradirin should be useful against methicillin resistant staph, see U.S. Patent 4,749,568.

• Known—Oxazolidinones adhere to intravenous (IV) bag.

» Novel–Oxazolidinones do not adhere to IV bag with 50% polyethylene.

◊ Nonobvious–No teaching in the prior art that 50% polyethylene would solve the problem.

- Known–Process at 0°–100°.
» Novel–Same process at 102°.
» Novel–Same process at 66°.

Surprising and Unexpected Evidence

What surprising and unexpected results do the two novel processes (above) produce? If nothing, then neither is patentable and both are not patentable. What type of evidence can be used to show surprising and unexpected results or properties? The answer is, anything. Examples below involve chemical processes and compositions.

With chemical processes, any of the following can be used to show surprising and unexpected properties:
Increased yield,
Shortened reaction time,
Expected side reactions do not occur,
An expected impurity does not result,
Can be performed in the presence of an agent that the prior art teaches will not work,
Expected destruction of functional groups does not occur,
Reaction can be performed with out heating,
etc.

With regard to compositions, more than just an additive effect is needed. For example, if a rust additive is added to paint and the paint does not rust, that is expected and not surprising and therefore not patentable. If a drought-resistant gene is added to a crop and the crop becomes drought-resistant, that is expected and not surprising and therefore not patentable.

Similarly if one were to make a composition of aspirin and decongestant X, if the composition did what was expected by stopping headaches/fevers and had decongestant action, that was expected and the composition would not be patentable. If however, the two ingredients were synergistic and the composition produced the desired results with less of each ingredient than expected, that would be surprising and unexpected and should result in patentability of the novel combination.

The fact that a product produces the expected qualitative effect does not necessarily negate patentability. In the 1970s and 1980s when the prostaglandins were the big new class of compounds, investigators realized that they were metabolized at the C-15 hydroxyl group, thereby inactivating them. It was apparent to the scientists that the oxidation of the C-15 hyroxyl group could be reduced substantially by forming a C-15 "blocked" compound. Because these were not metabolized as readily, they had increased activity which was surprising and unexpected. Hence, the claimed compounds were nonobvious and patentable.

After awhile the patent examiners realized that for whatever new series of prostaglandins was discovered, the C-15 "blocked" compounds would have more activity (expected). Therefore, even though these "blocked" compounds were more active, the patent examiners began rejecting them as obvious because now it was known (the prior art taught) by blocking the C-15 hydroxyl group the metabolic destruction of the compound would be slowed increasing its activity. Since the increased activity was expected, it was not surprising or unexpected. The rejection was valid based the *qualitative* knowledge that the "blocked" compounds are expected to be more active than the parent compounds.

With some prostaglandin inventions, the "blocked" compounds were outstandingly more active. In those situations, I made a *quantitative* argument. My argument was that the prior art taught/ expected the "blocked" compounds to be x% more active and acknowledged that novel "blocked" compounds that were not more than x% active were obvious within the meaning of §103. However, I entered evidence that the claimed compounds were substantially more active than x% and that was surprising and unexpected in view of the fact that they were only expected to be x% more active. The examiner withdrew the rejection and allowed my claims.

Be creative; if there are no qualitative differences, look to quantitative differences.

Since obviousness under §103 is the most difficult problem in obtaining patentability in most patent applications, before you request that a patent attorney draft a provisional patent application and file it, have the patent attorney do an informal[17] analysis of §103 in the same manner that a patent examiner will. Provide the patent attorney with (1) the closest prior art that you are aware of and (2) any surprising and unexpected results/properties of your invention. Having this analysis before you file should aid you in the decision as to whether you want to file.

Practical Aspects

There is a practical aspect to prosecuting a patent application with regard to the issue of obviousness that is not apparent but should be kept in mind. Often substantive prosecution of your patent

---

[17] I used the term "informal" analysis as opposed to a formal patentability opinion. The former is much less expensive, takes much less time and should give you the same answer. Some individuals, universities and businesses like formal written opinions for their files. You really don't need that; what you want is the answer.

application may not begin for almost four years after your provisional is filed.

If the patent examiner believes your invention is obvious in view of the prior art, in the first Office Action the patent examiner will reject the claims over one or more pieces of prior art. You will then have the opportunity to "reply" with or without amending the claims. In addition, you can submit evidence showing that the claimed invention has "surprising and unexpected properties" in view of the prior art. The "evidence" is usually a side by side comparison of your invention and the closest prior art. Submitting this evidence may mean doing additional research work if the particular comparison the patent examiner wants made, or you think should be presented, has not already been done. Sometimes the patent examiner will leave it up to you as to the exact experiment to conduct/compare, while other patent examiners may inform you of the comparison they want. In either situation experimental work may need to be done and submitted to the patent examiner by way of an Affidavit/Declaration.

Who will do the work? Has it been budgeted? Are the necessary resources including equipment available? Are the people qualified to do this work available and do they have the time?

Before having a patent application drafted and filed, consideration should be given to the "what if" issues. What if the patent examiner rejects the claimed invention as obvious and wants evidence of surprising and unexpected results before he/she will withdraw the rejection and allow the claims? Will there be someone to do the work and will the resources be available? Consider this issue before the patent application is drafted because if the evidence the examiner wants to see is not produced, the claims will be rejected again (final). I inform you of this potential problem because it is not uncommon for me to hear, "I can't do the work, I am on another project now," or "Sorry, I don't have the time," or "Sorry, it was not budgeted and we don't have the funds to . . . ."

§112 FIRST PARAGRAPH

Table 8 *(page 37)* alerted you that the first paragraph of 35 U.S.C. §112 has four parts:

- Written Description
- Teach one skilled in the art "how to make"
- Teach one skilled in the art "how to use"
- Best Mode

Remember that the "Written Description" requirement is something for the patent attorney to handle and nothing that you need to concern yourself with.

How To Make and Use

Teaching one skilled in the arts of how to make and use the claimed invention is something that you most likely will have to provide information to the patent attorney so he/she can draft the application. In most cases it will be easy for you to do since you are the one who made/conceived of the invention.

In situations where it is known how to make or use, that can be stated in the patent application instead of providing what is already known. For example, with the invention of using minoxidil for growing hair, it was known how to make minoxidil because it was on the market for hypertension. All that is needed to comply with "how to make" is something like, "It is well known to those skilled in the art how to produce minoxidil, *see* . . . [then cite a U.S. patent or journal showing how it can be made or is commercially available]."

Similarly, if one invents a better hammer out of a blend of metals which absorbs more of the shock so your arm receives less shock, you will have to teach how to make the new hammer. However, when it comes to teaching how to use it, something like the following is most likely sufficient, "The hammer of the present invention is used in the same manner and same way as the prior art hammers, as is well known to those skilled in the art."

As you can see this teaching of how to make and use may be quite simple. Generally you can provide a draft to the patent attorney and he/she will take it from there. In most cases one page will be adequate. Teaching how to make a new pharmaceutical is easy because the chemists have made it; we just use their experiment records. However, teaching how to use a new pharmaceutical can be difficult because most often at the time of filing of the patent application, no clinical trials have taken place. In fact, usually no animal experiments have even begun.

Best Mode

The "Best Mode" requirement means you cannot hide the preferred way of making or using the invention. It is inconsistent with a trade secret. One cannot patent a cola beverage and keep the preferred composition of ingredients secret.

What is the best mode of a process?
• The one that gives the highest yield?
• The one that is the cheapest?
• The one that produces the fewest environmental problems?
• The one that is the fastest to perform?
• The one that is patent free?

It is what the inventor considers the best (commercial) way to perform the process. Keep good notes so you can defend your reasons for selecting or not selecting various parameters for the best mode.

If the invention is a new process for stainless steel and it is operable from 25°–85°, and you know the best way to do it is from 48-53°, you need to point that out. My way would be to state, "the process is operable from about 25° to about 85°; it is preferred to perform the process from about 48° to about 53°."

If you are unaware of a preferred ingredients or conditions, that is not a problem. In the above situation the patent attorney would just state, "the process is operable from about 25° to about 85°."

One way patent attorneys used to invalidate patents during litigation discovery was to seek memos, notes, notebook entries, etc. and look for any that indicated that certain materials or conditions were preferred which were not disclosed in the patent. Many times during scale up or final development, engineers made minor but important changes that often did not get communicated to the patent attorney and therefore were *not* disclosed. However, the America Invents Act of 2011 eliminated failure to disclose the best mode as grounds for invalidity.

§112 - SECOND PARAGRAPH

The second paragraph of §112 requires the patent attorney to word the claims in a manner which particularly points out and distinctly claims the subject matter which the inventor regards as his/her invention. The claim language cannot be vague or indefinite. It insures that both the patentee and third parties know the limits of the claim.

Nothing for you to do here. Simple! Nevertheless, keep in mind the kinds of information that U.S. patents contain (Table 9).

Table 9. Organization of a United States Patent.

Component	Purpose
Drawings	Mechanical & Electrical
Background of Invention	
Field of Invention	For classification purposes
Description of Related Art	Prior art
Summary of Invention	§112 Written description
Description of Several Views (Drawings)	Mechanical & Electrical
Detailed Description of Invention	§112
How to make (Best Mode)	§112
How to use (Best Mode)	§112
Definitions	
Examples (Actual & Write-in)	Not required in U.S.
Charts	For chemical cases
Claims	Property rights
Abstract of Disclosure	Requirement

How Scientists Usually Get Patents

The usual procedure has three parts as follows:

1. Conception, the thinking part of an invention;

2. Reduction to Practice, the making of the invention. Constructive reduction to practice is the filing of a patent application *before* is it actually reduced to practice. More later on why this is sometimes done;

3. Submission of an Invention Report to a patent attorney, followed by many actions at various points in time (t).[18]

Time Markers for Important Actions

t = 0, the filing of a provisional patent application establishes the date of your invention for the material which is disclosed and adequately supported by teaching how to make and use. If some aspect is disclosed and it is not readily apparent to one skilled in the art how to make or use it, you will not get that date for the invention. It would be as if nothing had been filed.

Patents have a 20-year life from the date of filing the utility patent application. By filing a provisional prior to the filing of a utility patent application, the U.S. Patent will expire approximately 21 years from date of filing of the provisional. It does not increase the length of the life of a patent, it still is 20 years, but rather moves one year to the end where it is more commercially important and replaces the first year with the provisional year.

For some industries, such as electronics, technology improvements come very fast and the invention may be obsolete after 10 or even 5 years. In these situations the provisional patent application is not needed nor used. In other technology areas, such as pharmaceuticals which take many years to get to market, the year 20 to 21 can be extremely important.

Between t = 0 and t = 12 mo, additional provisionals can be filed if errors are found in the invention or additional scope or examples should be added. Usually none or one additional provisional is filed; the most I have filed is five.

---

[18] Small case "t" refers to time (days, months, years, etc.), not to be confused with an upper case "T" which refers to temperature.

The reason to file additional provisionals is, if you are adding new matter, you want the earliest date for that material.

t = 12 mo, the filing of an International Patent Application called PCT (Patent Cooperation Treaty) application and/or U.S. utility application.

If you invented technology which is likely to outdate in less than 20 years, you probably want to file your U.S. utility patent application at 12 mo to obtain a patent as soon as possible. Reasons for wanting a patent sooner than later is that you will then know (a) *if* a patent will be granted and (b) the *scope* of the claims.

If on the other hand, you are in an industry such as pharmaceuticals where you desire more time before you have to begin prosecution of your U.S. patent application, your patent attorney can file the PCT application at t = 12 and not file the U.S. utility patent application until t = 30. You will not get additional patent life; that date is determined by the filing of the PCT. You will still get the benefit of your provisional filing date. Doing it this way will give you an additional 18 mo to do additional testing to support patentability and learn whether the invention is as good as you originally thought. If not, you can abandon it to save prosecution expense.

Using the PCT route permits you to put off the filing of foreign patent applications until 30 mo. Some foreign applications can be filed and prosecuted in English such as Europe. However others, such as Japan, South Korea and China, require translation to the respective languages and obtaining local patent counsel in those countries. That can get expensive so it is best to wait to make sure that the invention merits the expense.

t ~ 16 mo, a Search Report and a Written Opinion should be issued by this time. The Search Report will inform you if the searching found any prior art more relevant than that which you submitted. The Written Opinion applies the documents found in the search to the claims on file. After the Search Report and Written Opinion, you will have a two-month period during which you will have an opportunity to amend your claims if necessary.

t = 18 mo, the PCT application is published. For individual inventors and small business, publishing the PCT application gives the world notice of your invention so businesses may come seeking a license. However, you do not have any allowed claims and may never have.

Possible competitors may now file information with the USPTO and oppose issue of your U.S. patent because, if allowed, it may give you a competitive advantage over them. They can also begin to market your invention since you do not have a U.S. patent with allowed claims. If a third party markets a product/composition and/or uses your process within the scope of the claims on file *and* those claims issue substantially unchanged, you can seek reasonable royalties for the use of your invention from the date of publication to the date of the issuance of the patent. If no patent issues, or a patent issues with claims that have been amended (narrowed) and no longer cover what the competitors are doing, they are free to continue to use what you disclosed but were unable to claim. They get a good head start.

t ~ 27 mo, decide in which foreign countries you want to try and obtain patents. Even though you do not have to file in the foreign countries until t = 30 mo, it takes time to translate your patent application. Most law firms have patent counsel that they are familiar with in virtually every country in which they have obtained patents, so finding patent counsel in each of the countries is not a problem.

t = 30 mo, file your patent application in each country in which you want to obtain a patent. Patent conventions permit in some cases one application to be filed for a number of countries which are geographically in close proximity. One application in the European Patent Office (EPO) will suffice for most all of the European countries. Your patent attorney will take care of these procedural matters.

If you did not file a U.S. utility patent application when the PCT was filed at t = 12 mo, it must be filed before the 30-mo deadline.

Prosecution Country by Country
After the 30-month procedural filing, prosecution begins in each country in which you have filed a patent application. Prosecution in each country is different and follows the rules and practice of that country.

Some Office Actions are procedural; some, substantive. Usually you get two or three substantive interchanges with the Examiner during and after which some claims may be allowed as filed, some may be amended to obtain allowance, some may be rejected final and you may cancel some. Claims that have been rejected final can either be canceled (if you give up on them) or appealed if you think the examiner is wrong and want another bite at the apple. When all claims remaining in a patent application are allowed, a patent will be granted.

It is possible to have all claims allowed or all rejected. Each patent application is very individualized and there are no general rules. I have done patent applications with one simple claim and others with more than 300 claims, sometimes with just one claim running more than five pages in length.

In the U.S., you can appeal the rejection of any claim to the Board of Patent Appeals and Interferences. If the rejections are affirmed, you can appeal further to the Court of Appeals for the Federal Circuit (a federal appellate court just one step below the U.S. Supreme Court). The America Invents Act of 2011 created post-grant proceedings in the Patent Office. So even if allowed, your patent could still be subject to legal proceedings at the USPTO.

Years ago in the U.S., once you obtained an issued U.S. Patent, your expenses were done. Not so now. Three times during the life of a U.S. patent (at 3.5, 7.5 and 11.5 years after issue), you have to pay maintenance fees to keep it in force if you wish to do so. If you no longer have interest in the claimed subject matter, you just don't pay the fee and the patent becomes inactive. Once you have stopped paying fees, the patent is no longer in force and you cannot later go back and pay the fees past due to reactivate the patent. So make sure you will not have future interest in the claimed subject matter before not paying the fees. Even if the fees are not paid and the patent is not in force, it is still prior art regarding future inventions. Foreign countries have various systems of yearly annuities or payments to keep patents in force.

Unlike real property which you can keep as long as you and your family want and until you sell, patents have a limited life of 20 years from the PCT filing date (about 21 years from the filing of the provisional patent application). In addition, a third party in a lawsuit can ask a court to invalidate your patent. If, after a trial the court agrees, your patent can be deemed invalid and you lose all rights at that time.

Considerations in Getting a Patent

What happens if two or more parties file for the same invention at the same time?

Until the America Invents Act of 2011, the law was (a) the US gave the patent to the "first to invent," and (b) all other countries gave the patent to the "first to file."

First to File was easy, fast to determine, cheap and without error. The Patent Office just looked at the filing dates and the one with the earliest filing date got the patent. First to Invent involved a very complex, time-consuming and terribly expensive procedure called an interference. Since interference practice disappeared in 2011, no more will be said about it.

If two or more parties now file for the same invention at about the same time, the U.S. also grants the patent to the first to file.

Coincidental Timing

It is not unusual for a number of parties to conceive of the same invention at the same time. I was involved in four- and five-party interferences dealing with classes of pharmaceutical agents called benzodiazepines and prostaglandins. There were four- party interferences dealing with the tetracycline antibiotics. This circumstance usually occurs when many people are doing research in a competitive hot area, such as erectile dysfunction (ED) or electrical cars, wind power, solar energy, etc.

The other situation occurs when people all attend a meeting in which new scientific information is disclosed. More than one attendee get the same idea. An example of this was a meeting between Pharmacia and Baylor College of Medicine to do a joint research project dealing with male contraception. After a full-day meeting discussing biology, chemistry, male physiology and past efforts, etc., the project leaders met with the top scientists. At the end of that meeting the question came up, "What compound(s) have the most promise and which one should we start with first?" Dr. J.B. of Pharmacia and the Baylor Professor looked at each other and both said, "Stanazolo methyl ether." So both scientists had exactly the same idea at the same time.

Assume we have a similar situation with Dr. Wise Willey and Dr. Untrained Underwood. Both go to a meeting, hear the same information. Both have a brilliant idea, go back to their respective employers, promptly go into their research labs, grab their research notebooks and write down the conception of the same invention.

The next day Dr. Willey goes to see the patent attorney at his employer, Smart Enterprises, and fills out an Invention Report form which asks the patent attorney to promptly file a provisional patent application. Dr. Underwood goes into his lab and immediately begins work on reducing his concept to practice. After four months of diligent work including a number of unsuccessful tries, Dr. Underwood proves it works. He records all the experimental work in his notebook and then prepares an Invention Report for submission to his employer's (Fly By Night Industries) patent attorney with instructions to drop all else and file this immediately.

Because the patent attorney at Smart Enterprises received the information months before the patent attorney at Fly By Night, he is able to file a provisional patent application for Dr. Willey two days before the same patent application is filed on behalf of Dr. Underwood. Result: Fly By Night did the work, but Smart Enterprises owns it. *The first to file owns the claimed subject matter.*

Recall, two of the requirements for patentability under 35 U.S.C. §112, first paragraph were (a) teach one skilled in the art "how to make" and (b) teach one skilled in the art "how to use." Notice there is absolutely no requirement to actually have made the invention or demonstrate that it is operable or works; only a requirement in §112 to teach one of ordinary skill in the art how to make and use the invention.

In many situations such teaching can be done with a fairly high degree of accuracy without actually having done the work. It does not take much time to write up an invention report, at most an hour. If that is done and the patent attorney starts work, you can go back to the lab and do the experimental work. If it does not work at all, the patent attorney can be told to stop work on patent application. If it works with modification, the new information can be given to the patent attorney and he/she can modify what they have started. If you believe others are working in the same subject area you are, it is important to be the first to file.

First to File Wins in ALL Countries
When I was responsible for Pharmacia's Alzheimer's chemical patents, I instituted a 48-hr rule. Once there was a conception, we filed a patent application within 48 hours. This was done because we were aware that others were working on the same subject matter that we were. The head of the scientific group agreed with me, if there was a choice as to be the first to make a pharmaceutical that stopped Alzheimer's disease or owning it, we would let others make it; we wanted to own it.

While it may seem strange that you can patent something that you have not as yet made, this is not new. In the museum at Kitty Hawk, North Carolina, a picture and a plaque honor those who made advances in aviation. One reads:

Hans-Joachim Von Ohain, Ph.D.
1911–1998
Developed the Engine Powering the
World's First Jet Plane

Hans-Joachim Pabst Von Ohain, Ph.D.,
patented a jet-propulsion engine in 1935
and continued to develop his design after.
He tested it on August 27, 1939, in an
experimental aircraft, the Heinkel He-178.
This was the world's first turbo-jet powered
flight. By 1942, a subsequent design was
powering the first operational German
fighter jet ME 262. Ohain would go on to
become Chief Scientist at Wright-Patterson
Air Force Base Aerospace Research
Laboratories.

Note that it states Dr. Ohain patented the jet engine in 1935 but did not test it until 1939. He may have done some work prior to filing a patent application, but he certainly realized the importance of first to file.

Even in situations where two or more patent applications are filed at about the same time for the "same invention," almost never is the invention exactly the same. What occurs is a substantial overlap of the claims. Although you are 100% sure others are working in the same subject area, it is impossible to know exactly what their claims would include when they file a patent application. It may overlap with yours (same invention) or just be close to it (different invention).

Let me make this very clear: I don't recommend filing before actual reduction to practice in most cases. It is the exception, not the rule. But if there is a concern that others may file on the same or very similar subject matter before you do, it is an option to be considered. It is not a legal decision since both methods are legal and it is not a technical decision. Therefore, it is a business decision.

Nomenclature of the Claims

It is useful to understand the nomenclature relating to the claims so you will better understand what your patent attorney means by what he/she says. There are "independent" and "dependent" claims, and they mean exactly what they say. Dependent claims are dependent on one or more independent or other dependent claims. Consider previous hammer examples:

1. A hammer having a head containing about 2 to about 8 % zinc.

2. A hammer according to claim 1, where the handle is of wood.

3. A hammer according to claim 2, where the wood is selected from the group consisting of oak, maple, pine, cherry and hickory.

4. A hammer according to claim 3, where the wood is oak.

5. A hammer according to claim 3, where the wood is maple.

6. A hammer according to claim 1 which contains about 3 to about 6% zinc.

These claims are relevant to a statement made about searching for freedom to operate. If you do not infringe an independent claim, you cannot infringe a dependent claim so you only have to search independent claims.

If during prosecution your independent claim is rejected and you cannot overcome the rejection and lose it, you will still have the subject matter of the dependent claims. Similarly if you lose an independent claim during litigation, you will still have the subject matter of the dependent claims.

An alternative system of nomenclature primarily used in chemical patent law is "genus" and "subgenus" pertaining to numbers of items:

- Genus claims refer to a large group

- Subgenus claim refer to a smaller group

- Species refers to one item

Comparison of U.S. and Foreign Patent Laws

The laws used to grant patents and what they must contain differ according to country (Table 10):

Table 10. Worldwide Patent Considerations.	
United States	**Rest of the World**
Filed in name of inventor	Filed in the name of assignee
First to file as of 2011 First to invent before 2011	First to file
Novelty, 1 yr grace period	Absolute novelty, no grace period
Term, 20 yrs	Term, 20 yrs
Provisional	No provisionals
Examples not required	Examples required, some countries

U.S. patent applications are filed in the name of, and for, the inventor. The inventor then assignees his/her rights according to his/her employment contract. Outside the U.S., the patent applications are filed in the name of the assignee.

Provisionals do not give an extra year of patent coverage; they just push back the 20- year term. Therefore, get the year that you lost up front at the back end where it may be more valuable depending on your industry. In industries where technology moves very fast, there is no need to file a provisional. Similarly with processes where technology moves very quickly, novel and better process replace processes in use long before patent life would expire.

Claim Examples

While the U.S. does not require examples (recall Table 9), most patent applications contain them because some foreign countries only give you what you can prove you have made. They usually accept examples in a patent application as sufficient evidence of what was actually done. If you have a constructive reduction to practice application and never made anything, in some countries you will not get a patent. Some countries and examiners permit data to be submitted later which was not originally in the patent application as filed.

Examples also help fulfill the requirement of teaching how to make and use. There are actual examples (things you have done) and write-in examples (things you have not done but consider important). Suppose you made the hammer with a oak handle but not with a maple one, the examples could read:

> Example 1.   Hammer with oak handle. (Give a detailed explanation of how the hammer was made and showing it works.)

Example 2. Hammer with maple handle.
          (Following the general procedure
          of Example 1, and making non-
          critical variations but using maple
          in place of oak, a hammer with a
          maple handle is produced.)

Example 2 teaches how to make the hammer of
the invention with a maple handle. No explanation
of how to use the hammer is required since it is
readily apparent to one skilled in the art.

IV.
HOW NOT TO LOSE YOUR PATENT RIGHTS

Some of the most tragic experiences in the technology business happen after this chain of events:

- An invention is discovered for something commercially important,

- Time and effort are spent developing the technology,

- Funds are spent drafting, filing and prosecuting patent applications,

- A patent is obtained in the U.S. and foreign countries,

- Investors realize both (a) the importance of the technology and (b) the protection from competitors offered by the patent so they invest funds for its commercialization,

- Capital is expended hiring people and/ or acquiring facilities to place the invented technology into commerce,

• Production and sales commence.

Only then does the assignee learn that either the patent is invalid or the wording of the claims does not prevent competitors from working around the claims.

That invention could be yours. The above scenario means that all the funds spent and effort expended to provide a 20-year period of exclusivity and protection for your invention are gone. It is as if you decided not to obtain any patents and donated all the money spent to some charity. This of course leaves you vulnerable to anyone copying your invention and competing with you. While you probably still have some advantage due to competitors' lag time needed to catch-up and gain "know-how," it leaves you in a very unenviable and vulnerable situation. Had the investors known this prior to their investing, it almost certainly would have caused them to by-pass your opportunity and invest their funds elsewhere.

Invalidity often occurs because the inventor violated one or more of the provisions of 35 U.S.C. §102 before filing the patent application or because of uncited prior art under §103.

Avoiding infringement occurs because the claims of the issued patents were not worded broadly enough to cover not only what the assignee desires to do, but also includes what competitors can do to use the "jist" of the invention without coming within the actual wording (scope) of any of the issued claims. The tragedy here is compounded by the following series:

1. Not only did the inventor/assignee think patent protection was assured,

2. He/she relied on thought when investing time and money in moving to the market place, but unfortunately

3. The claims were not worded broadly enough and

4. Competitors could use any and all information contained in the patent application for free.

Since under §112, the inventor(s) have to teach one skilled in the art how to make and use the invention including the best mode, now the competition has learned, and can use, the information the inventor(s) spent considerable time and money developing. This may permit the competitor(s) to undersell the inventor/assignee because the competitor(s) had little or no research or development costs. The inventor(s) will probably be at a significant competitive disadvantage compared to third parties who get all this information for free.

Invalidity of the Claims

The relevant law is 35 U.S.C. §102 Conditions for patentability; novelty and loss of patent rights *(italics added below)*:

A person shall be entitled to a patent unless—

(a) the invention was *known* or used by others *in this country*, or patented or described in a printed publication in this or a foreign country, before the invention thereof by the applicant for patent, or

(b) the invention was patented or described in a printed publication in this or a foreign country or *in public use or on sale in this country, more than one year prior to the date of the application for patent* in the United States, or . . . .

The phrases that are critically important are "known," "in public use," "on sale" and "more than one year prior to the date of the application for a patent."

With regards to §102(a), inventors often discuss the subject of their inventions with others of similar technical expertise and/or investors prior to filing a provisional patent application. That is good science and necessary for business. However, there is a right way and a wrong way to do the exact same activity. The wrong way is to do it without a Confidential Disclosure Agreement (CDA). You can make the exact same disclosure to the exact same people if you use a CDA because the information is confidential by agreement. If it is not confidential, then it is public or "known." It is that simple and any patent attorney can readily prepare an appropriate CDA for you.

With regards to §102(b), just make sure a provisional patent application is filed within one year of a sale, offering for sale or using the invention in public. Often individuals offer the product/composition/process of an invention for sale or use it in public either without knowing they need to file a provisional within one year or knowing they need to file a provisional in one year but for any one of a number of reasons the time goes by and they do not get it filed timely. Therefore, recommended procedure is to file a provisional *before* any sale, offer for sale or public use.

In addition, because the United States is the only industrialized country to have a one-year grace period with regard to novelty, and most of you will want patent protection in a number of commercially important foreign countries, you should file a provisional patent application *before* making a sale, quoting a price or using your invention in public.

If your patent becomes commercially important, competitors will search far and wide and in many different languages to find prior art (a) that you did not cite and (b) is more relevant than the prior art that you did cite.

If there is an item of prior art that you did cite but the most relevant part was missed or not appreciated by the examiner, the Court will take a second look and possibly invalidate one or more of your claims. Some patent attorneys try to slide close art by the examiner by either citing numerous documents so the examiner does not have time to thoroughly look for the most relevant part or if the most relevant part is in footnote or obscure place, not point it out to the examiner.

This may be good strategy to get you a patent in the short term. However, if your invention is important enough, a competitor will have scientists scour the documents you submitted looking for something the examiner might have overlooked. A better long-term strategy might be to point out the critical parts of all documents while prosecuting a patent application so you can rely on it with confidence when issued.

Competitors Use the Invention but Avoid Infringement

For the first few years of my patent work, I mainly drafted and prosecuted patent applications both in the Unites States and foreign countries on new products, pharmaceutical compositions and commercial processes. Because my Ph.D. was in fermentation chemistry I was given responsibility for "tin city," the company's chemical research, process chemistry and production facility. Most of the work involved drafting and prosecuting patent applications on commercial processes. One day management came to me with a competitor's patent on a process that was similar to one of our processes. They indicated that the competitor's process was probably better than ours and wanted to know if I could find a way to use the essence of their process without infringing their claims.

After thinking about it for awhile, I found a way to utilize the important aspect of their process without infringing any of their claims. From then on I was more careful in checking the claims I drafted because I knew how others would look at my patents and try and work around them.

Because I was successful in finding a way to use the essence of the competitor's patent without infringing it, management began bringing more competitors' patents to see if I could find a way to use their inventions without infringing any of their claims.

It is critically important that the claims be correctly worded with exactness. If they are too broad, the may well be invalid and if too narrow, competitors can work around them. The wording of an independent claim specifies the inventor(s)' intellectual property rights just as the wording of a deed specifies the owner's real property rights.

Before I give a few examples which are compilations of actual patents that I have reviewed to see if my client could use the invention without infringing any of the claims, I will illustrate with a real world situation where this occurs. This will help demonstrate how the "other side" operates and why correctly worded claims are so important.

The real world situation involves the federal Controlled Substance Act[19] which bans drugs such as LSD, heroin, MDA, methamphetamine, cocaine, psilocybin, etc. Drugs covered are categorized in Schedules. The government seeks to prohibit use by criminal law in a similar manner that a patent owner seeks to prohibit use (civil law).

---

[19] 21 U.S.C. §801, etc.

Schedule I[20] are substances that have no approved medical use, such as LSD, heroin and peyote. Schedule II[21] are items approved for medical use but under strict control including requiring all prescriptions to be written and no refills. Schedule III are items with less control. There are also Schedules IV and V.

Each schedule prohibits the use of particular chemical agents by designating them by name. For example, Schedule II includes the chemical compound N-[1-(β-phenylethyl)-4-piperidyl] propionanilide commonly known as fentanyl. It has the the following chemical structure (Figure 8):

Figure 8. Fentanyl Structural Formula.

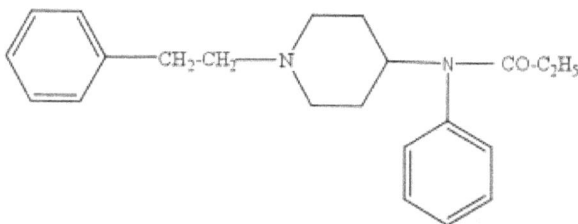

One of the golden rules of pharmacology is that compounds of similar chemical structure usually have similar pharmacological effects. We know that the class of compounds known as penicillins have antibacterial activity, the class termed benzodiazepines have anxiolytic activity, the class of steroids are hormones, etc. Fentanyl is a synthetic narcotic used for pain relief in cancer patients, following surgery, etc. "Underground chemists" believed this to be a profitable compound to make and sell. However, that would be a crime.

With this knowledge underground chemists as businessmen, not wanting to commit a criminal act but yet stay in business selling "fentanyl-like drug," made a "designer drug" of fentanyl

[20] 21 U.S.C. §812(c) Schedule I
[21] 21 U.S.C. §812(c) Schedule II

which has a very close chemical structure to the parent compound. It retains pain-relief activity but is a new and different compound which is not in the Controlled Substance Act, and therefore is not illegal! The first one they made was α-methylfentanyl (Figure 9) which has the following chemical structural formula:

Figure 9. α-Methylfentanyl Structural Formula.

Replacing one hydrogen atom (H) with a methyl group ($-CH_3$) creates a new compound with a

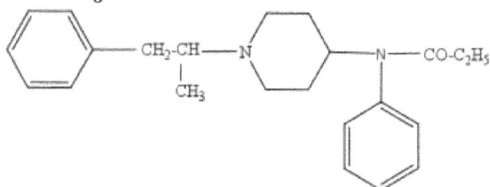

new name and new legal status that has similar chemical properties to the parent fentanyl compound. Since α-methylfentanyl was not a listed drug in the Controlled Substance Act, it was legal. Soon after the federal government found that α-methylfentanyl was on the street, they added it to Schedule I. So what would any good businessman do when his product is prohibited in the market? The answer is: find a new product to legally sell. Using their excellent business skills the underground chemists made another designer drug, *p*-fluorofentanyl (Figure 10), which has the following chemical structural formula:

Figure 10. *p*-Fluorofentanyl Structural Formula.

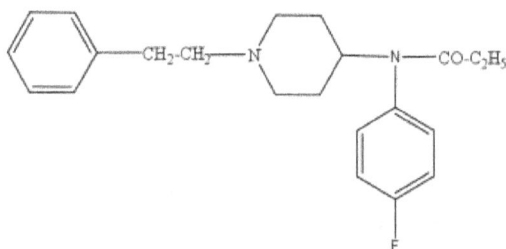

For this one, they just had to have a fluorine atom attached to the phenyl ring in the para (or 4-) position when this part of the molecule was incorporated during the synthesis. Since p-fluorofentanyl was not a listed prohibited item in the Controlled Substance Act, it was legal for a period of time until it was added.

So once an item is prohibited (made illegal) the underground chemists/businessmen not wanting to commit a crime, quit making the illegal substance and moved on to a new "designer drug." The exact same thing takes place in the civil arena with patents.

If a patent claim covers what you want to do, you avoid infringement, especially willful infringement and do your activity outside of the scope of the claim. What makes it harder to avoid infringement is that patent claims are much broader than the one item at a time under the Controlled Substance Act. Interestingly, the inventor of fentanyl patented (U.S. Patent 3,164,600) fentanyl to prevent unauthorized corporate pharmaceutical competition. He did include α-methylfentanyl in the broadest claim, but not p-fluorofentanyl. So with regard to the p-fluoro compound, the underground chemists/businessmen avoided not only the Controlled Substance Act but also the patent. You can see how easily this can be done.

The patent attorney seeking to prevent unauthorized use by pharmaceutical competitors in the broadest claim—claim 1—did not use the name, but rather included fentanyl in the chemical structural formula along with hundreds of other similar fentanyl compounds. Claim 1 reads:

1. A compound of the formula[22]

**Figure 11. Fentanyl-like Generic
Structural Formula.**

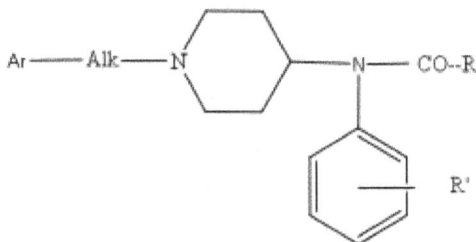

wherein Ar is a member of the class
consisting of
  cyclohexyl,
  phenyl,
  halophenyl,
  methoxyphenyl,
  aminophenhyl,
  nitrophenyl,
  pyridyl,
  furyl and
  thienyl;
Alk is a member of the class consisting of
  ethylene and
  propylene;
R is a member of the class consisting of
  lower alkyl,
  lower alkoxy,
  dimethylamino,
  cyclopropyl,
  morpholino,
  pyrrolidino and
  piperidino;
R' is a member of the class consisting of
  hydrogen,
  methyl and
  methoxy;
R" is a member of the class consisting of
  hydrogen and

---

[22] I have omitted an R" from the formula because it is totally
irrelevant to the discussion.

lower alkyl.

When Ar is phenyl, Alk is ethylene, R is lower alkyl, R' is hydrogen and R" is hydrogen, then the compound is fentanyl. In addition to fentanyl, the attorney also included many other chemically similar "designer drug" compounds because the inventor expected them to have similar pharmacological properties and knew pharmaceutical competitors would use them if not included in the claims.

When the government placed α-methylfentanyl (a designer drug) in Schedule I, the patent had already included that compound. When Alk is propylene rather than ethylene, the compound is α-methylfentanyl and is included in the scope of claim 1.

So patent claims prospectively can, and should, include what you think competitors would like to use of your invention. Unfortunately the Controlled Substance Act is retrospective and narrow; patent claims are prospective and broad.

Claim 2 is a subgeneric claim which includes fentanyl and claim 3 claims only fentanyl by its chemical name (just as the Controlled Substance Statute does). After the following examples, I will explain why this situation occurs and how you can prevent it from happening to you.

Claim Example #1
1. A process for the production of E which comprises:
    (1) stirring A + B to produce C;
    (2) isolating and purifying C;
    (3) heating C + D in a temperature range of about 30° to about 50° to produce E.

One possible way to use the process and avoid infringing the claim would be to use the process below 30° or above 50°. If too close to either 30° or 50°, it is possible that a judge would rule that, while there was no literal infringement, there was infringement under the DOE.

Another possible way to use the process and avoid infringing the claim would be to not stir A and B, but rather mix them. In this situation I had our production people specifically note in their procedure that A and B were *NOT TO BE STIRRED,* but only mixed. Bubbling an inert gas through a solution would accomplish mixing without stirring. I am sure the assignee would yell that mixing is an equivalent of stirring and seek to have the DOE applied. It is doubtful that they would succeed.

Still another possible way to use the process and avoid infringing the claim would be to omit step (2) if it did not decrease the yield too much. It is preferable to isolate and purify C before reacting with D. In some reactions, almost no product would be obtained if you did not isolate and purify C before continuing, but in other cases it would only reduce the yield a few percent. The scientists would have to do the experiment and determine how much decrease in yield result if step (2) is omitted. If it does not decrease the yield substantially (or less then the cost of a license), then this is the way to go because the DOE is not applicable to the omission of a step.

The way claim 1 should be worded to avoid these problems is:

1. A process for the production of E which comprises
   (1) contacting A + B;
   (2) contacting the product of step (a) with D.

    2. A process according to claim 1 where the
    product of step (1) is isolated and purified.

"Contacting" includes both stirring and mixing. Further, whether or not a third party isolates and purifies C, they infringe redrafted claim 1. If the "best mode" is to isolate and purify C, then it should be included as a separate dependent claim, claim 2.

Claim Example #2
The patentee has successful product "D" but later finds a better way to make "D" by the process of A → B → C→ D. The patentee files a new patent application claiming the three-step process which issues with the following claim:

    1. A process for the production of D which
    comprises
    (1) transforming A → B
    (2) transforming B → C and
    (3) transforming C → D

This process is diagramed below:

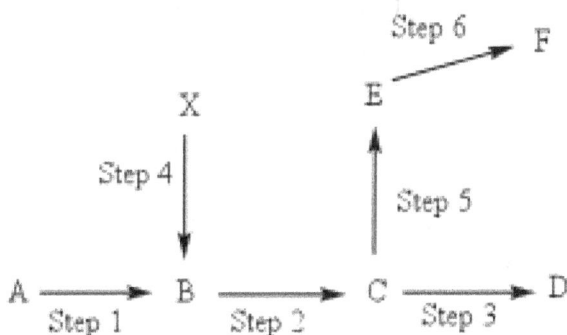

One way to use much of the process and not infringe the claim would be to start with another compound that will also produce B but by a different method. If X can be transformed to B by the process of Step 4, then one can do Step 4, Step 2 and Step 3 and not infringe the claim.

Whether D is an antibiotic, or plumbing joint lubricant or a soldering compound, if F is different, but similar enough to do the same job (maybe not as well, but acceptable), then another way to use much of the process and not infringe the claim would be to do Steps 1 and 2 of the claimed process but then do Steps 5 and 6 to produce F. This does not infringe the claim because the claim requires Steps 1, 2 and 3 be performed.

An alternative way to use Steps 1, 2 and 3 to produce D without infringing would be for a third party, Cheatum Chemicals, to use Steps 1 and 2 to produce C, but not Step 3 producing D. Instead our savvy business, Cheatum Chemicals would then sell C as a bulk product. A fourth party, Stealing Sales, would then purchase C and convert it to D by the process of Step 3. Neither Cheatum Chemicals nor Stealing Sales did Steps 1, 2 and 3 so neither infringes the claim.

To prevent all these possible problems what the patent attorney should have done was use three simple independent claims such as:
> Claim Step 2, [B → C] as a single step
> Claim intermediate B
> Claim intermediate C

If the claim was to just Step 2, the transformation of B → C, any of the proposals for working around the three-step claim 1 would be infringing. Similarly infringing, if the claim was just to intermediates B or C.

Claim Example #3

A chemist who is an expert with polishes invented a "color restorer" for addition to normal car polish which will restore the car's finish to near new. He filed a patent application and licensed it to Super Polish, Inc., a company that specializes in car and boat polishes. In due course a United States patent issued and was assigned to Super Polish, Inc., which began to manufacture and sell its product.

The main competition for Super Polish, Inc, was Cheatum, Inc., which is a very aggressive company in attacking competitors' patents, but is very careful to do only lawful activities to avoid charges of "willful infringement."

A summary of the invention, the prior art and two separate formulations which the assignee perfected, as well as the claim the assignee obtained after prosecution, are all set forth in Table 11:

Table 11. Novel Car Polish with "Color Restorer."				
Item	**Prior Art**	**EX1**	**EX2**	**Claim**
Cleaner	Y	10	5	3-25
Color Restorer	No	15	20	10-30
Buffer	Y	5	5	3-10
Polish	Y	10	15	5-20
Wax	Y	50	50	40-65
Inert	Y	10	5	qs[23]

Since the color restorer is not in the prior art, the car polish composition was patentable. The two formulations which the assignee developed are EX1 and EX2. Since each of the ingredients is operable at amounts above and below the highest and lowest amounts tried, the patent attorney correctly drafted the claims broad enough to include other operable ranges.

Cheatum, Inc., showed the issued United States patent to their patent attorney and instructed her as follows:

- We want to market a car polish and advertise that it contains the new "color restorer" and in

---

[23] Means an amount sufficient to bring the composition up to 100%.

an amount sufficient to restore a car's finish to "like new;"

• We do not want to infringe any claim of Super Polish's issued United States patent and

• Please gives us two alternative formulations that will not infringe Super Polish's patent and which contain the color restorer so we can use their invention to compete against them.

To analyze the situation, Cheatum, Inc's patent attorney made the following chart:

Table 12. Cheatum's Patent Attorney Analysis.			
Item	**Claim**	**CHEATUM-1**	**CHEATUM-2**
Cleaner	3-25	10	10
Color Restorer	10-25	20	20
Buffer	3-10	5	0
Polish	5-20	2	10
Wax	40-65	50	50
Inert	qs	13	10

She told Cheatum, Inc's legal and business units that neither formulation CHEATUM-1 nor CHEATUM-2 literally infringe the claim.

Formulation CHEATUM-1 does not literally infringe because the amount of Polish is only 2% whereas the claim requires 5–20%. However, it is possible that a court could find that this formulation infringes under the DOE.

Formulation CHEATUM-2 does not literally infringe because it contains no Buffer. Further, because the Buffer is required by the claim, a court cannot find this formulation infringes under the DOE. Cheatum, Inc., can correctly advertise that it contains the same Color Restorer, and same amount, as does Super Polish's new product.

How and Why Do These Situations Occur?
They occur for a couple of reasons:

1. It is virtually impossible to proofread your own work because you are too close to it.

2. The focus of all involved parties—the inventor(s), business people and patent attorney—on the product/composition/ process being contemplated for development. Certainly that needs to be included and is quickly and easily done. However, the focus really needs to be on how will competitors try and use the invention and side step coming within the wording of the claim. Inventors and their business management almost never focus on that aspect when reviewing a patent application. They usually want to make sure what they want to do is covered. That is essential and easily done.

   However, they must take the next step to make sure competitors cannot work around their claims. After all, a patent does not give the assignee the right to use the claimed invention; only the right to exclude others. The assignee needs to make sure competitors *are excluded.*

The patent claiming VIAGRA Tablets, a well-known ED pharmaceutical, only needed one claim to one compound to protect what it was going to market. There were only 58 compounds exemplified so the assignee was going to select one of these. However, the focus was correctly not on the 58, as it was quick and easy to protect these in a claim. Rather the generic claim includes well over 1,000,000 compounds; *see* U.S. Patent 5,250,534. Why? Because the assignee wanted to make sure that a competitor did not select any of them to compete with the compound they chose to market. Well done.

3. The ego of the patent attorney in not needing help.

What You Can Do To Prevent This Problem?

Very simple. Just do the review I do to use an invention without infringing, but do it *BEFORE* the patent application is filed. I do it after the patent has issued.

What you need to do is have an "appropriate individual" carefully examine each independent claim before the patent application is filed to see if that individual can find a way to use the invention without coming within the scope of the wording of any of the independent claim(s). If he/she can, then the claim needs to be broadened to include the activity that would permit someone to use the invention without coming within the wording of the claim.

The "appropriate individual" needs three basic qualifications:

1. Have good understanding of the technology involved,

2. Have a reasonable understanding of patent claims and

3. Be unfamiliar with this particular invention before being asked to review the claims.

If the person is not well technically trained in the subject matter, he/she may not realize ways to work around the claim wording or alternative ways that are operable and not infringing.

If the person is not well-versed in understanding how claims operate, they will not be able to distinguish infringing from noninfringing activity. They will not sufficiently understand what is required of them.

If the person is familiar with the invention, they tend to read over obvious holes. We are all familiar with the situation that it is much easier to proofread and find errors in work that we are not familiar with than our own work.

Suitable individuals include people like these:

Patent attorneys who work in the area of technology but have not previously seen this patent application,

Retirees who have worked in the same area of technology and who have had some patent experience and

Professors who work in the area of technology and who have had some patent experience.

The cost is minimal since only about an hour of time is required. Compared to the tens of thousands of dollars you will have invested in the patent process, an hour of consultation is a very cheap insurance policy.

V.
ENFORCEMENT OF
PATENT RIGHTS

If someone steals your car (personal property), you call the police (government) to catch the thief and hopefully get your car back. If someone is trespassing on your land (real property), you contact the police (government) to enforce your real property rights. If someone is infringing one or more claims of your patent (intellectual property) and you call the police, they will inform you that the government is not involved in enforcing intellectual property rights; you as patent owner have to enforce them yourself.

Each country issues its own patents and has its own laws. No jurisdiction enforces patent laws; that is something the owner (or licensee if so specified in a license agreement) has to do in each jurisdiction that they have a patent which is being infringed by a third party.

In the United States patent infringement is covered by 35 U.S.C. §271(a) which reads in relevant part, ". . . whoever without authority makes, uses, offers to sell, or sells any patented invention, in the U.S., during the term of the patent, infringes the patent." So the acts of infringement are making, using, selling and offering for sale. Third parties are free to write about, discuss, etc., a patented invention.

The legal action the patent owner has against a third party who is infringing is civil, not criminal, and takes place in the federal court system. The trial is in the U.S. District Court of appropriate venue. These lawsuits are very time-consuming and expensive.

Defenses to Infringement Actions

The defendant has defenses to patent infringement actions. These are noninfringement and/or invalidity of the patent. Often the defendant will use both defenses in the alternative. They will answer that they are not infringing the patent but if they are, the patent claims are invalid. The burden of proof is on the patent owner to prove the defendant is either literally infringing one or more claims of the patent or there is infringement under the DOE. Since patents have a statutory presumption of validity, the burden of proving invalidity rests with the defendant. Each claim of your patent is presumed valid independent of the validity of the other claims.

Since infringement and validity are all or nothing issues, if the case is not settled there is one winner and one loser. If a patent has 20 claims and a defendant is able to avoid infringement of 19 or have those 19 invalidated so he only infringes one claim, he is still infringing and the remedies are the same. So the only "out" for a defendant in a patent infringement action is to avoid infringement of *all* claims or have all the claims which are being infringed, judged invalid.

Since those involved in the business end of patents do not like the all or nothing outcomes, not infrequently patent lawsuits are settled before the trial begins. Often they are settled during the trial as both sides hear the evidence presented, but before a verdict is reached with the patentee granting the "alleged infringer" a license in exchange for a royalty. That way both are still involved commercially. The patentee gives up the chance for getting the "alleged infringer" off the market and having the entire market for patentee in exchange for royalties and preventing of the risk of losing the patent. The "alleged infringer" gives up the possibility of being able to compete with the patentee without any payment in exchange for a guaranteed spot in the market and the protection of the patent from other competitors in exchange for the payment of royalties.

The remedies available to a patentee which prevails in a lawsuit are (1) injunction and (2) payment of damages. Should the patentee be able to prove the infringement an "exceptional case" which usually means willful infringement, the Court can increase the damages to triple and also require the losing party to pay the patentee's attorney fees.

An injunction prevents the defendant from infringing again. If they do, they then have to answer to the court, not just the patentee. It is not wise to anger a Federal District Court judge by violating an injunction.

Damages are to compensate the patentee for lost profits. The measure of damages is the lost profits of the patentee, not the profits of the infringer. In an Arkansas case I had, the defendant proved that he was making about $1 profit/unit. My client proved our lost profits were $4/unit. Because my client was able to prove the infringement was willful and the court found it was an "exceptional case," the court doubled the damages to $8/unit and required the defendant to pay my client's attorney fees.

The patent statute limits the patentee's damages to going back six years. If you believe someone is infringing a patent you own, promptly contact your patent attorney to make sure you file a lawsuit within six years. In addition, you want to make sure the party that may be infringing is aware of your patent which gives you a chance at recovering increased damages and attorney fees.

The patent statute requires you to mark your product/composition or product of a process with the relevant patent numbers to give the public notice that your product/composition or product of a process is protected by a patent.

There are some very practical issues that you need to be aware of. I have been amazed at the number of times experienced individuals have overlooked some of these issues by asking these questions:

Q: How do you enforce a process patent for a staple item of commerce?

Q: How do you enforce a patent which claims a method of screening?

Q: How do you enforce a patent in countries which do not honor patent rights?

Q: How do you enforce a patent which can be practiced in international waters?

All of these questions are answered with great difficulty! The last issue was overlooked by a major research university. They came to me wanting a patentability opinion as to the likelihood of obtaining a patent. I told them they were asking the wrong question. I asked them, even if they could obtain a patent, how would they enforce it? They informed me, they never thought of that.

In all of these situations, serious thought should be given to *not* filing a patent application to protect the intellectual property. Alternatively, I suggest you give serious consideration to trade secret protection. Many very valuable inventions, including Coca-Cola™, are protected by trade secret protection rather than a patent. One big advantage to trade secret protection is that it does not expire in 20 years, but continues on indefinitely as long as the secret is kept.

How Does the "Research Exemption" Work To Protect Against Enforcement?

The simple answer is that there is no statutory or case law exemption for "research." Some believe that "de minims" (trivial, insignificant or technical) infringement is not actionable, that too is incorrect. While there is no research exemption in law, in practice one does exist. The following example will show how it works.

Suppose there are ten auto makers all competing in the market and patenting new improvements so they could be the only ones in the market offering the newly invented item. There are two different common scenarios. One is where the patented item comes on the market about the time the U.S. patent issues. The other is where the patent issues long before the item is placed in the marketplace.

An example of the former is when Awesome Auto develops a device which monitors wind speed and direction as well as air density and automatically adjusts the fuel usage for the most efficient use, resulting in significant dollar savings to the car's owner. Due to significant prosecution issues, the U.S. patent does not issue until the same year as the first model year when Awesome introduces an auto with this device.

The nine competitors want to learn about the device, test it to see how it works and then "invent around" it so they can develop their own similar noninfringing device. They could follow Awesome's disclosure under §112 where they are required to teach one skilled in the art how to make and use the invention. However, most of the nine decide it would be faster and cheaper just to purchase one auto to get the device. Awesome having sold a vehicle with the device can no longer charge infringement for "use." Hence, by purchasing a vehicle with he device, a competitor is free to do research and experiment with it.

An example of the latter is when Careful Cars develops a device which monitors the driver's eye movements. Should it appear to the device that the driver is dosing off, an alarm sounds which ensures the driver will not fall asleep. Due to development caution in making absolutely sure the patented device works 100% of the time, the product does not appear in an auto sold by Careful Cars until five years after the patent issues.[24]

As soon as the patent appears the other nine auto makers wanting to learn about this new item so they can "invent around" the patent, make and test the item following the §112 disclosure in the patent. By making and testing in the item, they are "making" and "using" the patented item without authorization; the nine companies are committing acts of infringement. The fact that the "making" and "using" is for research purposes does not avoid infringement.

The reason these acts of infringement do not result in lawsuits seeking (1) an injunction and (2) damages is two-fold. First, with regard to

---

[24] With pharmaceuticals, often the patent issues 5–10 years prior to the patented product.

infringement, each of the companies infringes each others' patents for the same purpose—research. Would Awesome sue Careful over the anti-sleep patent and then Careful sue Awesome over the gas saver? And each of these sue the other eight? No. The real reason is (b) no one was damaged. Neither Awesome nor Careful lost sales of a vehicle due to these acts of infringement.

So while there is infringement on a very small scale, there are no damages and hence no lawsuits. This results in a practical "research exemption" which is why so many believe there is a statutory or judicially-created research exemption in the case law.

VI.
Expenses

Patent expenses can best be divided into two groups, statutory fees and attorney fees. When filing, prosecuting and maintaining patent applications and patents in foreign countries, you will find each country has its own fee schedule.

The United States statutory patent fees are set forth in 37 C.F.R. §1.16 and can be found at *http://www.uspto.gov/web/offices/ac/qs/ope/fee100512.htm*. Notice that the U.S. has three different fees for each item: the standard "fee," a Small Entity Fee and a Micro Entity Fee. For any fee, the Small Entity Fee is 50% of the standard fee and the Mirco Entity Fee is 50% of the Small Entity Fee (25% of the standard fee).

Generally, if you are not hired to invent, meaning your employment contract does not require you to assign or license any patentable invention to your employer, you qualify as a Small Entity. Non-profits also qualify. Information as to who else qualifies is found at 37 C.F.R. §1.27(a)(2)ii). It also includes the statement, "Questions related to standards for a small business concern may be directed to: Small Business Administration, Size Standards Staff, 409 Third Street, SW., Washington, DC 20416." So if you have any questions, you know whom to contact.

Most patent attorneys work on an hourly basis. Their hourly rate may differ for different types of patent work such as drafting patent applications, writing briefs or arguing appeals. In addition to the hourly rate, a patent attorney or law office may have standard charges for routine items to cover clerical help in processing the documents.

Probably the easiest way to get a ballpark estimate of the costs involved is to trace the path of an invention from the time you contact a law office until the patent expires. The figures (Tables 13 and 14) are just very rough estimates to give you an order of magnitude. I will not include any information regarding patent litigation since that is beyond the scope of this book.

Table 13. Ballpark Estimates of Attorney Costs.	
Item	**Expense (U.S. Dollars)**
Prefiling	0 – 5,000
Infringement Opinion	0 – 4,000 or more
Informal[25] Patentability Opinion	0 – 1,000
Formal Patentability Opinion	0 – 5,000 or more

Prefiling includes conferences whether in person or on the phone. It can also include legal opinions such as an infringement opinion as to whether your invention might infringe an issued patent. More likely it will include an informal patentability opinion. Since the cost of a formal patentability opinion (which could be wrong) is approximately the cost of filing a provisional and PCT patent

---

[25] I used the term "informal" analysis as opposed to a formal patentability opinion. The former is much less expensive, takes much less time and should give you the same answer. Some individuals, universities and businesses like formal written opinions for their files. You really don't need that; what you want is the answer.

application, many prefer to request an informal opinion. Then, if positive, file a provisional and PCT applications to see what the International Search Report and Preliminary Examination as well as the first U.S. Office Action says on the merits.

Table 14. Ballpark Estimates of Selected Filing Costs.	
Type of Filing & Associated Fees	**Estimated Cost (U.S. Dollars)**
Provisional Filing (t = 0)	2,000 – 10,000
Provisional filing fee[26]	130[27] or greater
Attorney fee	2,000 – 10,000
PCT Filing (t = 12 mo)	
PCT[28] International fee	Approximately[29] 4,000
United States Utility filing fee	140 or greater
Attorney fee	0 – 8,000

A provisional patent application does not need to include claims nor prior art and can be a much simpler patent application so the attorney

---

[26] It is easy enough to set forth the United States statutory fees as they are, as of the day I am writing this. However, from time to time Congress increases and adds fees. I could just set forth the particular part of 37 C.F.R. § which is applicable as of the date of writing but this can also be changed by the USPTO. I don't want to make the reader research each and every fee as they read. It will be helpful to the reader to know the order of magnitude of the fees; is it about $10, about $100 or about ??? Therefore, I will use the fees that are presently in force with the statement "$xx or greater." That will be a correct statement and give a ballpark idea of the fees.

[27] See 37 C.F.R. §1.16(d). This is the Small Entity Fee, the regular Fee is $260. All fees set forth will be the Small Entity Fee.

[28] PCT has only one standard fee. There is no Small Entity Fee.

[29] This depends on whether the PCT application is filed in the United States receiving office or a foreign one. Since the fee includes the International Search and Preliminary Examination, some prefer to have this not done in the United States. If filed outside of the United States the currency conversion to Euros also is a factor.

fee starts as low a $2,000. The purpose of a provisional is to permit the applicant to file quickly and cheaply and to be able to get an early date. Basically all that is required for a provisional patent application is to meet the requirements of 35 U.S.C. §112, teach how to make and use and provide a written description so that is it apparent that the inventor has a complete invention.

Some attorneys, for various reasons, prefer not to file a bare bones provisional but file a complete patent application. They do this because, if no additional information is found or generated regarding the invention, the provisional will in essentially be identical to the national-phase utility patent application.

Let's assume it will cost $7,000 to file a complete national-phase utility patent application. If the patent attorney files a bare bones provisional patent application, the attorney's fee may be only $2,000. Later when upgrading the provisional to a full national-phase utility patent application, the patent attorney's fee would probably be about $5,000 to make the total about $7,000. In the situation where all the information was available and the attorney chose to do a complete patent application for the provisional, the attorney's fee for the provisional would then be $7,000. When it came time to file the PCT/national-phase utility patent application, the patent attorney's fee would be approximately zero. So in both cases the total patent attorney's fee is about the same.

Many inventors and most universities prefer to do the bare bones, cheap, provisional patent application because, if at the end of the year they decided not to go forward with a PCT/national-phase patent application, they will have saved about $5,000. That happens when (1) additional data shows the invention does not have the commercial potential originally thought or (2) the assignee tries to license it and realizes the market is not there.

The difficulty that often occurs in doing the bare bones provisional with the idea of completing and/ or adding to it in 11 months is that time to finish the patent application comes up scarce. Maybe the same patent attorney is no longer with the firm and someone has to start over or there is no one now at the firm with the expertise with the particular technology involved. Problems occur on the assignee's side as well. Sometimes the scientists involved leave the company or switches to a new position within the same company and no one familiar with the experimental data and prior art is available.

Unless there is a good chance that a PCT/ national-phase utility patent application will not be filed, I think it is preferable to file as complete a provisional as possible. If more data comes along in a few months that the assignee wants included, a second or third provisional can be filed. The fee is nominal and it takes very little time to add experimental data or modify something found to be in error.

By filing just a provisional patent application and a PCT patent application you are able to file both in English, hold your original provisional filing date as your patent date for every country in the world and get almost to t = 30 months before spending big money. I say "almost" because the national-phase applications have to be filed by t = 30 months and it takes a few months to get a foreign agent and translation (Table 15). So your decision as to which countries you want to go foreign in should be made by about 27 months.

Table 15. Timing and Fees as Filing Factors.

Document Type	Approx. Timing	Associated Fee
Publication	(t = 18 mo)	None
International Search Report	(t > 18 mo)	Paid with PCT filing
Preliminary Examination	(t > 18 mo)	Paid with PCT filing
National-phase filings	(t < 30 mo)	
Varies by language and length	"	Translation
Varies by country	"	Statutory filing
Varies by country	"	Foreign patent agent
Necessary for Coordination	"	U.S. patent attorney

By 27 months you should have a very good idea if you will be able to out license, assign or sell your patent applications or in the alternative commercialize it your self. If you cannot commercialize your invention in any manner, the PCT patent application can be abandoned with no additional expense. Normally you only go forward from here if commercialization is a real probability one way or another. I call the above "foreplay" because to this point you probably will have a rather minimal amount (about $7,000 to $15,000) invested in the patent process.

Starting at about 27 months, foreplay ends and we get down to serious business. Some counties in a geographical area can be prosecuted in one application such as the EPO (European Patent Office which covers the European countries). However, if you want to have patents in other industrialized countries, such as Japan, China, Korea, Israel, etc., you will need translations and patent agents in each of those countries. In addition, patent agent expense in those countries will begin as prosecution moves forward. If the EPO patent is granted, you will then need translations for each of the European countries, such as Germany, Spain, France, etc.

So starting at about 27 months patent application expense is considerable and you need to seriously consider whether the investment is likely to be worthwhile. Holding your priority date for over two years in all countries of the world for about $7,000 to about $15,000 is a great deal.

Maintenance Fees

The cost of going from 27 months to obtaining patents in many counties of the world and then paying maintenance fees or annuities to keep them alive can easily run to $100,000 or more depending on many factors.

In the United States once you obtain your patent, your expenses do not end. If you wish to keep the patent in force for the 20-year period from the earlier of the date of your PCT or United States national-phase patent application (about 21 years from the priority date of your first provisional),[30] you need to pay maintenance fees at 3.5, 7.5 and 11.5 years of $800, $1,800 and $3,700, or greater, respectively. If the patent is providing exclusivity to permit you to commercialize your invention sufficient to make these payments a cost of doing business, great! If not, you cannot make the payment and effectively dedicate the patent to the

---

[30] After filing your provisional patent application, there are two different ways to file your U.S. national-phase patent application. One is at the same time the PCT patent application is filed. The other is not to file when the PCT is filed (t = 12 mo), but wait and file it as a national-phase patent application at 30 months just as a national-phase application can be filed in Japan, European Patent Office, Korea, China, Australia, etc. Often this decision is dictated by the technology you are involved in and the stage of development.

public. Once the patent is not in force, you can not reactivate it.

The long and short of expenses is you can buy up to about 27 months or a little longer for a nominal amount. Starting at that time, expenses increase greatly. Given that it takes a few months to usually file a provisional patent application, you will have about two and a half years to license or commercialize your invention before expenses begin to jump. Then you should decide whether to proceed with prosecution or abandon the patent application.

Most inventors and business people think that it is much easier and quicker to out license an invention than it is. My recommendation is to give yourself plenty of time, so start as soon as your provisional is filed. Recall at this point you do not have a patent, may never get a patent and if you do get one, you do not know the scope of the claims that will be allowed.

Now get up and walk around the licensing table to the position of the potential licensee. If you were the potential licensee, how much would you be willing to pay for something that may never be or if it is, you don't know either the scope or value of it? Given that precarious position, a potential licensee will want the time for its patent attorney to thoroughly study the patent application, the prior art, the claims on file and other items before rendering an opinion on the likelihood of obtaining a patent in any industrialized country. That opinion will also include the probable scope of allowed claims. In addition to this legal study and opinion, the business unit of the potential licensee will need time to evaluate your submission from their perspective.

VII.
DISCLOSURE OF PRIOR ART

What Is Prior Art?

Prior art is what your invention is measured against both for novelty and obviousness. It includes, but is not limited to, U.S. patents, foreign patents, research journal articles, trade journal articles, newspapers, theses which are catalogued, books, oral presentations (at technical and professional meetings), seminars, advertising, promotional pamphlets, etc, etc. Anything in any language which is public before your filing date is prior art to you.

Legal Duty To Disclose Close Prior Art to the USPTO

Because patent applications are prosecuted *ex parte,*[31] there is a legal requirement to disclose prior art that is "material to patentability." 37 C.F.R. §1.56 is the Duty of Candor and Good

---

[31] *ex parte* means "from one party." With patent applications there is no party on the other side as in litigation where there is both a plaintiff and defendant. The inventor applies to the government (the United States Patent and Trademark Office) for a patent.

Faith. It requires an applicant for a patent, as well as the applicant's attorney to disclose to the USPTO any information known to them that may be material to the issue of patentability. Failure to do so may result in severe penalties, including unenforceability of the patent.

The applicant must have clean hands and not hide prior art that is relevant to the claimed invention from the patent examiner so the claims can be examined over the closest prior art. You have no duty to search for prior art, but you can't hide what prior art you are aware of. There is an affirmative duty under the law to disclose the closest and most relevant prior art you are aware of to the USPTO. Not doing so could cause loss of all patent rights.

Besides the legal duty, a very real practical reason exists to submit all relevant prior art you are aware of to the USPTO. Patents have a presumption of validity. Hence, a third party in court trying to assert that your patent is invalid has a high level of proof required to invalidate it. However, if the patent has not been examined over the particular piece of prior art the third party is asserting and the judge determines it is more relevant than the prior art the examiner reviewed, the presumption of validity is lost and the level of proof required to invalidate the patent is less. You don't want that to happen to you.

It is not prudent to conduct research and development work, invest precious financial and human resources, go into production, do marketing and creating a market only to find the patent you are relying on for protection from competitors is invalid. Unfortunately this happens too often.

Prior art may include the video of a oral presentation at a professional society meeting or the abstracts of a technical meeting that are not available by an Internet search. If you are aware of such prior art and it is unlikely the patent examiner will find it, you could be tempted to not produce it and hope the patent examiner will not become aware of it. Don't yield to the temptation; you want to make sure the patent examiner has a copy if you believe the item discloses information that is material and/or relevant to your invention.

How the Patent Examiner Uses Prior Art

The patent examiner first determines what is being claimed in the patent application. Next the patent examiner determines where your patent would be classified (class/subclass) *if* a U.S. patent is granted. After that, the examiner searches that class/subclass and similar classifications to see what is the closest prior art. In addition, the examiner probably will do an electronic search for non-patent documents as well.

Years ago before electronic searching, not too rarely the applicant and patent examiner found different prior art and it was not uncommon for the patent examiner to miss a significant document. However, with electronic searching and the experience of examiners, they are not only likely to find the same prior art but more. This partially occurs because of their experience in working in the technology subject area and also because they may have access to data bases that the applicant does not. This will include data bases of foreign documents.

After the patent examiner has determined what he/she believes is the closest prior art, the patent examiner checks (1) to determine whether the claimed subject matter is novel (§102) and if it is, then (2) to determine whether the claimed subject matter is obvious (§103) in view of the prior art.

With regard to obviousness, the patent examiner can combine references. For example if your invention is a hammer with a oak handle and the patent examiner has one document that discloses hammer with maple, cherry, pine or walnut handles and a second document disclosing axes with oak handles, the examiner may reject the claims as obvious over the first document in view of the second document.

How Inventors Disclose Prior Art to the USPTO

The inventor is required[32] to file an Invention Disclosure Statement (IDS) which is a list of prior art items[33] that the inventor believes to be material to patentability.

The items disclosed in the IDS can also be set forth in the Background of the Invention section (refer to Table 9, page 59) and briefly discussed there. Most attorneys do not do this. On the other hand, some attorneys not only discuss documents, but provide a fair amount of additional "background" information.

In addition, if the attorney wishes to discuss one or more prior art documents, they can file a communication under 37 C.F.R. §1.2, which is one way not to put the information into the patent application file and communicate it to the patent examiner.

The IDS must be filed. An inventor only needs do that and many/most law firms that *only* do that. However, there are different ways to do an

---

[32] 37 C.F.R. §1.97–1.98

[33] Most prior art is usually "documents" such as U.S. and foreign patents and scientific journal articles. I use the broader term "items" because it includes not only documents but also other things that are art prior art, such as videos of oral presentations, CDs of talks, program posters, pamphlets of organized professional meeting, etc.

IDS or provide information in the Background of the Invention. Since different ways are legal, then which way to do it is not a legal decision for the attorney. Nor is it a technical decision for the inventor/scientist. Hence, it is a business decision for whoever is making those decisions with regard to the patent application. Unfortunately most often those who can and should be making the decision rarely are aware of that important fact. My experience is that no patent administrator at any university that I have worked with was aware that this was a business decision for them. They routinely left it to patent attorney to decide.

Further, you can use different ways for each of these methods to comply with the duty of candor and good faith. Therefore, it is important for you to understand the differences between them and why one might select one method and not another. If you had more than one invention and the any of the facts including the nature of the prior art, the industry, potential commercial value, etc., were different, you might select a different method. Three methods (A–C) with their numbered variations include those outlined below:

Method A. IDS Required

1. IDS "naked," as the bare minimum, just a list.

2. IDS to hide or bury a document. If you have two documents which are very close, relevant and/or material to the claimed invention and you don't want the examiner to find them, submit them along with about 30 others and place them at #17 and the other at #25 it is less likely the patent examiner will realize the significance of these two.

3. IDS to avoid critical information not readily apparent. If the critical portion of the document is small, such as a sentence

or two or a footnote, even if only a few documents are listed, it is unlikely the patent examiner will have the time to read each document thoroughly and critically and find the important information.

Method B. Background of the Invention (a patent application section)

1. Nothing, occasionally little or nothing is here.

2. General background information, but no discussion of items in IDS, is quite commonly done.

3. One sentence describing the document and one sentence distinguishing the claimed invention. This is what I do in most cases and will explain why below.

4. A more thorough discussion of the document; best not to do. Wait for a rejection and then respond if necessary; if no rejection, the information was not needed.

Method C. Communication under 37 C.F.R. §1.2

This way the information is not in the patent application, not provided to patent examiners in foreign countries and primarily used if the prior art is only relevant in the U.S. or you do not want to make it available in general and provide it on a country by country basis. However, once a patent issues the entire file is open to the public and anyone seriously interested in the invention will eventually find this information.

Which Is the Best Way To Disclose Prior Art to the USPTO?

I will give a typical lawyer's answer, "It depends!"

Working through two common situations I will call S1 and S2 may be the best illustration. In S1 your searching finds about 25 documents that generally deal with the invention. Ten of the 25 are the closest to the claimed invention, but are not really very close at all and none are highly relevant. In this situation has no problem and most patent attorneys disclose just the ten. The method used for disclosure is rather unimportant because none is really material to patentability.

In S2 you find 25 documents; seven are reasonably relevant and two are very close to the claimed invention. Reviewing the two with your patent attorney and other patent attorneys in the patent attorney's law office, opinions split evenly as to whether the claims should be allowed in view of the two very close important documents. How many of these documents do you include in your IDS? Twenty-five? Seven? Just two? What is the best method to disclose these documents? There is no question that you have to confront the issue of obviousness head-on at some point.

With S2, the method you choose probably will depend on when and where you want to confront the issue of obviousness. The factors that influence which method pursued usually depend on a number of issues including whether the decision maker is a law firm, and whether the client is a large corporation or a small business/inventor.

There are two common methods of disclosure. One I will call Patent Office (complete disclosure) and the other Court (minimal disclosure). Each method looks to confront the issue of obviousness in these different venues. The two methods can best be compared in tabular form, but these points summarize the extent of disclosure effects in Tables 16 and 17:

- Likelihood of patent issue, a major concern of the law firm because they want satisfied clients, as well as your concern

- Strength of presumption of validity, your concern

- Your ability to license, your concern

- Royalty amount, if any, your concern

- Downstream expenses, your concern

Table 16. Disclosure Methods in Confronting Obviousness.

Disclosure is	Minimal	or	Complete
METHOD known as	Court		Patent Office
. . . .			
REASON to use	Better chance for patentability in USPTO		Want determination both fast and cheap prior to investment
. . . .			
RESULTS wanted Presumption of Validity	Weak or none		Strongest

---

So since when the prior art is very close, the extent of disclosure is critically important to you. You should make the decisions on how you want it disclosed. By the way you disclose the prior art, you have influence on whether the fight over patentability/obviousness takes place in the USPTO or in the courts.

Table 17. Advantages and Disadvantages of Disclosure Methods.

Method	Advantages	Disadvantages
Patent Office	Cheap Fast Board of appeals has technical expertise Have determination early Easy to license Should obtain higher royalty	May lose patent rights

Court	Obtain a patent
	  (presumed valid)
	Ability to use "muscle"
	Forces challengers
	  into court
		Cost of litigation
		
		Time of litigation
		Uncertainty
		  exclusivity
		Difficulty to license
		Reduced
		  royalties

The Complete Patent Office Disclosure Method

With the Patent Office path, the applicant confronts the issue of obviousness head-on in the patent office itself by making sure the patent examiner is aware of items critical to patentability (usually obviousness, but can be to prior use or prior sale, etc.). Having done so, if the patent is granted, it is very unlikely a court would again consider the issue of obviousness with regard to the items "laundered" at the Patent Office.

Norml patent prosecution involves the Patent Office path where all issues of patentability are thoroughly covered in the USPTO, including obviousness with regard to each item that is relevant. Using the Patent Office method one probably would include only the seven most important documents in the IDS (Method A.1). My practice is then to utilize Method B.3 to set forth in the Background of the Invention a brief description of each document in just one or two sentences followed by a sentence distinguishing the claimed invention. This establishes novelty and leaves only obviousness on the table for the examiner to consider.

For example: *Popular Mechanics* 37, 231–233 (2008) disclosed hammers with handles of oak, cherry and maple. The handles of the hammers of the invention are only walnut. Or if the key information is very minimal and the patent examiner is likely to miss it, I would say something like the following, "U.S. Patent 1,234,567 discloses a car polish composition containing 20-40% abrasive. Column 14, lines 26–33 mentions that less abrasive should be operable. The present invention uses only 11–14% abrasive."

In the first example, it is clear that the hammers of the invention are novel, the hammers of the identified document do not have handles of walnut; novelty is established. Both the prior art and invention are hammers with wood handles— close prior art. It is then up to the patent examiner to decide to reject the claims as obvious or allow them. The issue is confronted. If the patent examiner allows the claims, they have been reviewed over the closest prior art and it is very unlikely that a court will again consider this issue over that particular document. If a third party finds a item of prior art that is closer, maybe hints at a walnut handle or states all hardwood handles are equivalent, then the court might review again.

If the patent examiner rejects the claim, the applicant can appeal to the Board of Patent Appeals. This Board consists of three "judges" who were experienced patent examiners, who are very familiar not only with technical subject matter but also the patent laws. An appeal is relatively cheap because it is an appeal and not a trial; there is no discovery and there are no witnesses as in patent litigation since all the evidence is already in the record. Further, your patent attorney already has all the arguments for patentability and knows from prosecution why the patent examiner is rejecting the claims. If the patent examiner is citing case law, usually it is only one or two cases.

Further, even though a patent examiner can participate in the appeal[34] and argue against patentability, in the 15 or more appeals that I have argued I don't recall a patent examiner ever participating. Lastly, often the appeal is determined on briefs only without oral argument. Even with oral argument, the patent attorney only gets 20 minutes and the patent examiner 15 minutes[35] (if they participate, which is rare). The appeal is a very short, extremely inexpensive compared to a trial and the legal procedure is very simple. All of this results in a cost that is a small fraction of the cost of litigation.

So the Patent Office path is cheap, fast and if you prevail, you have a patent which most likely will not be challenged over this item of close prior art. In addition, your patent will have a strong presumption of validity in court. Further and very importantly you have a high degree of certainty with regard to the validity of this patent and can therefore move forward on the business side with confidence that you have patent protection to protect your product, composition or process. Competitors who study the situation thoroughly will realize it is a strong patent and have no choice but to obtain a license if they wish to use the patented product, composition or process. In addition, and very importantly you can request, and probably get, a royalty at the high end of the

---

[34] 37 C.F.R. §41.47(d)
[35] 37 C.F.R. §41.47(d)

usual royalty range because the third party has
no good alternative.

The big downside is you could leave the appeal
process with no allowable claims and therefore
no patent. However, if the claims are obvious you
will likely lose them anyway in court litigation
when validity is challenged on the grounds of
obviousness. Especially for individual inventors,
small businesses and universities, it probably is
best to know this before you invest substantially
in the business end. Using the court method you
would not have this certainty until years after an
appeal would have taken place in the USPTO.

The Minimal Court Disclosure Method
With the Court path, the applicant attempts to
avoid having the patent examiner consider the
critical documents. He/she realizes that it is very
likely subsequent litigation will occur in Federal
District Court in which the issue of invalidity
is raised over the two key items of prior art.
By selecting the Court path, the applicant is
indicating a preference for fighting the obviousness
issue in court rather than the USPTO. This route
gives major corporations with deep pockets an
advantage over small businesses which do not
have the experience, revenue or muscle for major
litigation.

Courts, whether state or federal,[36] do not like
technical issues because the judges are not
technically trained. In addition, they rarely get
patent cases and are not familiar with either the
substantive laws regarding patent issues or the
procedural laws regarding patent litigation. Judges
are much more comfortable handling business
contracts, criminal matters, tort law, etc.

---

[36] All patent litigation involving issues of infringement and
validity are in the federal court system.

The Court path attempts to avoid dealing with the issue of obviousness during prosecution in the USPTO and does so by obscuring the critical documents. Utilizing this approach, the IDS is filed as Method A2 or A3. Under S2, the IDS A2 would list all 25 documents found and sprinkle the important seven and critical two in the list and not differentiate them. In the Background of the Invention, Method B1 or B2 would be utilized. Using B2 would possibly distract the patent examiner and take up some of the patent examiner's time normally used for examination of the prior art.

The objective of this path is obtaining a patent regardless of whether it is of dubious validity. The patent that issues will have a presumption of validity until some third party convinces a judge during litigation that the patent examiner did not appreciate the importance of the two critical documents. The major advantage of this approach is that the applicant is more likely to obtain an issued U.S. patent.

The list of disadvantages (Table 17) are major disadvantages for individual inventors, small businesses and most universities. However, they are less a disadvantage for large corporations that have the experience, money and muscle to keep the patent alive. Even some small businesses can operate with a patent of dubious validity if their licensees and competitors have less experience, money and/or muscle than they have.

To challenge a important patent against a large corporation could cost several million dollars and take a few years of time. Not many individual inventors, small businesses or universities are willing to take on this commitment unless the subject matter is extremely important to them *and* they have the budget and personnel to handle such a major undertaking.

A reasonable number of issued U.S. patents subject to litigation are held invalid by courts. With others when push comes to shove, the assignee decides it is not worth the time and expense to defend especially when there is a good chance it will be held invalid. Often these patents are ultimately are involved in a license deal having a low royalty. For the assignee/licensor some income is better than no income and you still have the patent to fend off those who are not very aggressive. These situations are never reported so the actual number of invalid patents is unknown and can only be estimated by those who are involved in licensing and litigation.

Method Choice Depends on Who You Are
For small businesses, individual inventors and most universities, I strongly recommend the Patent Office path. I do so because it is unlikely that these assignees will be able to commercialize a patent of dubious validity either by actual working the patent or by out licensing. If these entities are able to get allowable claims and an issued U.S. Patent, they then are much more willing to invest in production and commercialization or able to find parties interested in licensing the patent and at a fair or better royalty.

This results because the assignees know that if there is a challenger, their patent has had a thorough review and therefore a strong presumption of validity which gives them a good chance to prevail in court. If some entity forces the issue by infringing and makes you sue them, they run a reasonable risk of being held to be willful infringers which can be very costly.

Large corporations have the muscle to commercialize a patent of dubious validity. Personally, I don't like the uncertainty that goes with it, but I am not a poker player either.

I previously indicated that one of the factors that seems to influence which path is taken is if the decider is a law firm. Virtually all law firms take the Court path to get a patent at all costs for the client, even if it is of dubious validity. They realize that if a battle over obviousness is to be fought it will be fought it in the courts, not in the USPTO. This is not at all bad for the law firms and could be interpreted as very self serving. Besides getting you a patent, if you get into litigation, who are you going to turn to? Yes, turn back to your patent attorney with more business for the law firm.

Further, assume you are new in the research/ invention patent business and you inquire of two friends who have had extensive experience with patent law firms. One, Liberal Lew, uses the limited disclosure and "Court path" and the other, Conservative Charlie, who decides to go with a fuller disclosure, the "Patent Office path." Assume that of 10 patent applications filed, eight are clearly allowable, one is probably allowable 55/45 and the tenth is probably not allowable 55/45. Let's see the results (Table 18) of each:

Table 18. Hypothetical Results for Limited vs. Fuller Disclosure.		
Item	Liberal Lew	Conservative Charlie
Patent apps. filed	10	10
Applications paid for	10	10
Patents allowed	10	9
Patents paid for	10	9
Appeals in USPTO	0	2
Possible litigation	2	0
Licensable patents	9	9
Expense	Much more	Much less
Uncertainty	Yes re #10	No

Now if Lew tells you his patent law firm got him 10 issued U.S. patents from the filing of 10 U.S. patent applications and Charlie tells you his patent law firm could not get allowance of all 10, then had to appeal two and lost one, which firm would you think did the best job and which would you choose?

It sounds like Liberal Lew has the better law firm. That may be fine if you are a large corporation. However, those of you reading this most likely are sole inventors or from small businesses. Lew paid for 10 patents, but can only commercialize nine. If there is litigation on the two that are questionable, Lew will have to pay for two trials, probably winning one and losing one. Patent litigation is very expensive and time-consuming tying up resources. Lew will spend much more and have less certainty. His company may be able to recoup the expense if they have sufficient muscle to deter litigation and force a settlement. If not, Lew will spend more money and be in court while Charlie will be relaxing on the golf course.

Having written patent applications as a ghost writer for patent law firms that retained me, I've seen this firsthand. One way or another I usually know who is the law firm's client. Typically I have no direct contact with the actual inventors or their business people, all communication goes through the law firm. When I submit the patent application to the patent law firm, usually only one thing gets changed: the firm deletes my Background of the Invention (B3) and replaces it with a general discussion (B2). This has happened even in a situation where the prior art is as close as can be and an obviousness rejection is certainly expected *IF* the patent examiner finds the important document and the critical part. The very important documents will be buried in the IDS between a number of other documents of no importance.

How the prior art is presented to the USPTO is not a legal decision for the patent attorney or law firm, but rather a business decision for you to make. Review the prior art, your invention, your likely competitors, the importance of the subject matter, your litigation budget, etc., and make whatever decision is best for you at that time.

VIII.
AMERICA INVENTS ACT OF 2001

This Act of Congress made a number of changes to our patent law. However, most of these are issues that your patent attorney needs to be aware of, not you.

If two or more parties file patent applications claiming the same invention and assuming that the subject matter in both applications is patentable, who gets the patent? The answer to this question was the biggest change to American patent law incorporated into the America Invents Act of 2011. It is something that you need to know.

Prior to the America Invents Act of 2011, the answer to the above was the first to invent under 35 U.S.C. §102(g). The answer now is the first to file. So it is imperative not to delay filing your patent application if you believe that someone else might be working in the same technology area.

IX.
SELECT TOPICS

Invention – Something new, not necessarily patentable. A six-legged chair is probably an invention since it is novel. It will not be patentable because it is obvious.

Conception – The thinking part of an invention.

Reduction to practice – The doing part of an invention. Actual reduction to practice is making the invention and realizing it works; it does not have to be optimized. Constructive reduction to practice is the filing of a patent application after conception without an actual reduction to practice.

Inventorship – In foreign countries a patent application is filed in the name of the assignee, not the inventor. In the United States, the patent statute requires that a patent application must be filed in the name of the inventor(s). Since this is a legal determination it will be made by the patent attorney drafting the application. Since it is the inventor of the claims, the patent attorney will not know who is and is not an inventor of the invention until the claims are finalized. It is not the same as determining whose name goes on a paper about the invention to be published.

Years ago prostaglandins were the subject of many patents. Most prostaglandins had the top side chain as Δ5, so when someone conceived of Δ4-prostaglandins that was an invention. The usual bottom chain was a straight-chain alkyl group of eight carbon atoms. So when someone else conceived of 17-phenyl for the bottom chain, that was also an invention.

One day an excellent chemist, Dr. M, conceived of Δ4-17-phenyl prostaglandins and entered the conception into his notebook. He stated what was well known to those skilled in the art how to make this invention because each of the side chains was already known. Further, he stated that they would be used by methods well known to those skilled in the art—the same as other prostaglandins. Management wanted him to work on a different project and assigned the project to a different chemist, Dr. R.J.

Dr. R.J. in due course made and tested the compounds, and an Invention Report was filed Even though Dr. R.J. did all the work, it was determined that Dr. M was the sole inventor since Dr. M had a conception of the complete invention and Dr. R.J. was in essence just a pair of hands. A paper was written and submitted to a journal; the sole author was Dr. R.J.

Research Notebooks – Prior to 2011, it was very important to record a conception and any work towards reduction to practice in a research notebook. The reason was in case more than one patent application claimed the same invention, the patent application of the invention was placed into an interference. The research notebook contained the evidence needed to prove the dates of conception and reduction to practice. Since interference practice was eliminated in 2011, the need for recording the information is less. Should there be a claim that you derived (stole) the invention from someone else, having a research notebook showing the dates of conception and the dates of work you did will be very helpful in showing the date on which you had the invention.

Invention Report – The information that I request from inventors is in the form set forth in Appendix B.

Trade Secrets – Just what it says. A secret, it is disclosed only on a need to know basis. Once it is public your competitive advantage is lost. While patent protection is limited to 20 years, trade secret protection is indefinite.

Obviously trade secret protection is not useful for products or compositions that can be reverse engineered easily. Coca-ColaTM is a composition that has been kept as a trade secret because no one has been able to successfully reverse engineer it exactly. Some have come close. Trade secrets are best used for processes that are unlikely to be discovered by a third party and novel microorganisms.

Trade secrets are inconsistent with the best mode requirement of the patent law. You cannot hide the best way of making the invention.

Term – Both the United States and foreign countries have a 20-year term from the PCT or national filing date, which ever is first. Because the United States permits the use of provisional patent applications, the term is about 21 years from the date of the provisional patent application if one is filed.

GLOSSARY

C.F.R. refers to Code of Federal Regulations, these are administrative rules. 37 C.F.R are the rules that refer to patents.

MOT refers to Method of Treatment which is a patent claiming a "process" of treating a human or useful warm blooded mammal.

MPEP refers to the *Manual of Patent Examining Procedure*, the 8th edition of which issued in August 2001. The MPEP is a manual published by the United States Patent and Trademark Office (USPTO) for patent attorneys/agents as well as patent examiners. It includes all the statutes (laws) and regulations that are followed in the examination of U.S. patent applications.

PCT refers to the Patent Cooperation Treaty, an international treaty regarding the filing and prosecution of patent applications in other countries around the world.

Rx refers to pharmacy, pharmaceutical, etc.

Specification is the non-claim portion of the patent application.

U.S.C. refers to United States Code, federal statutory law. Title 35 U.S.C. is the federal statute regarding patents.

USPTO refers to Untied States Patent and Trademark Office.

USEFUL USPTO WEBSITES

The USPTO website
http://www.uspto.gov/

Patent Laws 35 U.S.C. §
http://www.uspto.gov/web/offices/pac/
mpep/consolidated_laws.pdf

Code of Federal Regulations for Patents;
37 C.F.R. §
http://www.uspto.gov/web/offices/pac/
mpep/consolidated_rules.pdf

Manual of Patent Examining Procedure (MPEP)
http://www.uspto.gov/web/offices/pac/
mpep/index.html

To do a search at the USPTO
http://patft.uspto.gov/

Classes and subclasses of patents at the
USPTO—once a class is selected you will be
taken to the subclasses of that class
http://www.uspto.gov/web/patents/
classification/selectnumwithtitle.htm

Patent fee schedule at the USPTO
http://www.uspto.gov/web/offices/ac/qs/
ope/fee031913.htm

APPENDIX A

ISOMERS as MIRROR IMAGES

An asymmetric center is a carbon atom with four different groups (such as R, Q, X and Z) attached producing two enantiomers (isomers), one "left handed" and one "right handed" which are mirror images of each other. The plain lines are in the plane of the paper, the dotted line is behind the plane of the paper and the wedge is in front of the plane of the paper. The two are mirror images of each other and no matter how you rotate or twist they are not superimposable; they are different. One will rotate plane polarized light to the right and the other will rotate it to an equal degree to the left.

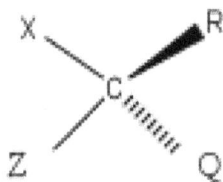

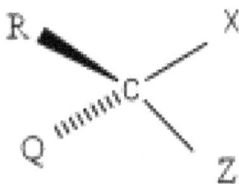

APPENDIX B

INVENTION REPORT CHECKLIST

1. What is old (prior art)?
    a. YOU have an *affirmative duty* under the law to disclose the closest relevant prior art that you are aware of. *NOT DOING SO COULD CAUSE LOSS OF ALL PATENT RIGHTS.*
    b. Have you provided two (2) copies of all relevant non-US patent references?
    c. What are the most relevant references? What may be the most relevant (closest references) is a matter of judgment and interpretation. The Patent Office's conclusions may be different than yours. Therefore, if in doubt whether or not to disclose a particular reference, it is recommended to error on the side of disclosure.
    d. Please give a one sentence summary of the relevancy of each references and a second sentence distinguishing the claimed invention. A hypothetical example appears below.

    The *Journal of Fun Chemists*, 123, 4567 (1899) discloses:

. . . indoles directly attached to a steroid at the 2-position of the indole and the 21-position of the steroid. The invention claims indolyl-linker-steroids where the indole is attached at the 5-position to either the 11- or 21-position of the steroid by a $-CO-$ or $-CH_2-$ group.

2. Novelty
   What is new (invention)?

3. Obviousness
   a. What is surprising and unexpected about the invention in view of the closest prior art?
   b. What problem does the invention solve that the prior art does not?
   c. Why should the invention be patented?

4. Have you set forth:
   a. "how to make" the invention, if not well known to those skilled in the art?
   b. "how to use" the invention, if not well known to those skilled in the art?

5. Have you set forth the "best mode" of your invention as you **now** know it at the time the invention submission is being made? Should the "best mode" change before the filing of the patent application, even if by another scientist, you must update your submission.

6. Have you set forth a scope of your invention, *i.e.,* things that you may not be particularly interested in commercializing but that you don't want your competitors to have?

7. All submissions to the attorney should be in electronic format to facilitate prosecution.

APPENDIX C.

THE MOST IMPORTANT STATUTES

35 U.S.C. §101, Inventions Patentable. Whoever invents or discovers any new and useful process, machine, manufacture, or composition of matter, or any new and useful improvement thereof, may obtain a patent therefore, subject to the conditions and requirements of this title.

35 U.S.C. §102, Conditions for patentability; novelty and loss of right to patent. A person shall be entitled to a patent unless

a. the invention was known or used by others in this country, or patented or described in a printed publication in this or a foreign country, before the invention thereof by the applicant for patent, or

b. the invention was patented or described in a printed publication in this or a foreign country or in public use or on sale in this country, more than one year prior to the date of the application for patent in the United States, or

35 U.S.C. §103, Conditions for patentability; non-obvious subject matter. A patent may not be obtained though the invention is not identically disclosed or described as set forth in section 102 of this title, if the differences between the subject matter sought to be patented and the prior art are such that the subject matter as a whole would have been obvious at the time the invention was made to a person having ordinary skill in the art to which said subject matter pertains. Patentability shall not be negated by the manner in which the invention was made.

35 U.S.C. §112, Specification. The specification shall contain a written description of the invention, and of the manner and process of making and using it, in such full, clear, concise, and exact terms as to enable any person skilled in the art to which it pertains, or with which it is most nearly connected, to make and use the same, and shall set forth the best mode contemplated by the inventor of carrying out his invention.

The specification shall conclude with one or more claims particularly pointing out and distinctly claiming the subject matter which the applicant regards as his invention.

ABOUT THE AUTHOR

Bruce Stein, R.Ph., Ph.D., J.D., is a registered pharmacist, has a Ph.D. in fermentation chemistry and is an attorney. As an attorney, he practiced patent law for The Upjohn Company, Pharmacia and Upjohn and then Pharmacia for 25 years. He then practiced part-time representing mostly universities, small businesses and individual inventors.

While in industry he was involved in drafting and prosecuting over 200 patent applications both in the United States and world wide. In addition, he has handled over a dozen appeals to the Board of Appeals, a few interferences [under 35 U.S.C. §102(g) which were eliminated by the America Invents Act of 2011] and numerous license agreements.

While at Pharmacia his main focus was obtaining patents for novel compounds useful for pharmaceutical purposes, but he also was responsible for patenting new processes to produce known chemical agents as well as new pharmaceutical formulations for known pharmaceutical agents. In addition, he has patented microorganisms and novel crystal forms of compounds.

The above activity was to obtain patents for Pharmacia. In addition, Dr. Stein represented the Fine Chemical Division of Upjohn (*see* Preface) and "worked the other side of the fence" in that he was responsible for avoiding or invalidating competitors' patents. Learning how to avoid infringing the claims of competitors' patents taught him how to better draft his patent applications so competitors could not avoid infringing the claims in the patents for which he was responsible.

Intellectual property includes patents, trademarks, copyright, trade secrets and the Plant Variety Protection Act. Dr. Stein used trade secret protection when the subject matter could be better protected by that form of intellectual property.

He also represented The Asgrow Seed Company (a subsidiary of Pharmacia) and participated in about 40 lawsuits under the Plant Variety Protection Act. He submitted briefs on behalf of Asgrow and argued the *Asgrow v. Winterboer* case at the Court of Appeals for the Federal Circuit. When the case went to the Supreme Court, he managed the case there where Asgrow prevailed 7-1.

INDEX

Note: The italic letters *f, n,* or *t* following a page number indicates a figure, note, or table on that page. Double italic letters mean more than one such item on a single page.